BLESSED TO BLESS
LOVED TO LOVE
LED TO LEAD

By: Dr. Ed Delph

Blessed to Bless … Loved to Love … Led to Lead
There's a Leader in You Who's Dying to Lead Others Through You
By Dr. Ed. Delph

ISBN 978-1-4675-6582-0

First Print 2013

Nationstrategy
7145 W. Mariposa Grande Lane
Peoria, Arizona 85383
USA

This book is dedicated to the country of Australia, the Great Southland of the Holy Spirit, that I believe has blessed the world with leaders and leadership for such a time as this. Every time I am in Australia I am inspired, especially by many of the emerging church leaders in the nation, who will not settle for second best.

CONTENTS

Introduction

I don't know what leadership is. You can't touch it. You can't feel it. It's not tangible. But I do know this: You recognize it when you see it.
—Bob Ehrlich

I have never written a book on the subject of leadership. For years, I have admired the authors who have, like John Maxwell, Ken Blanchard, Larry Kreider, Alan Platt and a host of others. I think former Maryland Governor Bob Ehrlich captured the essence of leadership perfectly when he said, "You can't touch it. You can't feel it. It's not tangible. You recognize it when you see it." [i]

This book is a series of verbal snapshots on leadership. The thoughts come from newspaper articles that I have written in my weekly newspaper column called "The Church-Community Connection." These articles reach thousands of people each week. You can't write about God without writing about leadership. God is the ultimate Leader. He created leadership and He creates leaders.

All who are Christians have The Leader of leaders inside them. That Leader is wanting, willing and waiting to come to lead others through you. You have it in you. Let it out of you. That is what being salt and light is all about.

Rick Joyner, founder and director of MorningStar Ministries, once said that you can either use leadership or be used by leadership. That is a great statement. You use it or you lose it. Someone is going to lead and it might as well be you. Each one of us has a sphere of influence that needs the Leader in us. Be the change!

In this book, I have tried to avoid the seven-steps-to-leadership type of approach. This is not that kind of book. My purpose is to introduce you to what leadership looks like, what if feels like to you and others, and to show you leadership in action. The book will inspire you, equip you, and demonstrate leadership in action to you. It is about catching the "vibe" of leadership. It will give you a leadership reference and help engage the Leader in you for the benefit of others.

So, onward, upward and outward! Welcome to a bigger world! You've got mail — wake up … shake up … put on your makeup!

Ed Delph

Chapter 1

Change Is Such a Constant that Things Are Constantly Changing

If you take care of your team of employees during the transition, your employees will take care of your customers and your customers will take care of your business.

Edward Deming said the following on the subject of change: "You don't have to change. Survival is not compulsory." That caught my attention.

A few days ago, I was speaking in Kuala Lumpur, Malaysia. I was asked by a company in the insurance industry to speak on the subject of change. The owners of this successful business were in the process of making some strategic decisions and changes that positioned the company for success in the future. My assignment was to prepare and present a paper to the owners and to all of their employees on why they were making the changes and what the process would be to go through the change.

I started by asking the owners of the company the following questions (which they approved) in front of the company's employees:

"The world today is in amazing times. Things are changing fast. What do you anticipate changing in our industry in the near future?"

"What do we need to do now to position ourselves for success and sustainability in the future?"

"Our company has been on a wonderful journey so far. In your opinion, where are we vulnerable?"

"What are we doing well and what could be do better?"

"What specific changes should leadership consider for success in the future?"

"How will these changes for the future benefit all of us?"

"How can the employees help in making these changes?"

"What preparations have you as owners made for us all to transition effectively with as little discomfort as possible?"

"If someone gets frustrated, angry or fearful, or is intimidated during this change process, what can he or she do and who should they talk to?"

That is quite a list of questions, isn't it? But this is real life and real life goes best when there is good change management. Information is motivation. Pastor Jason Arant notes that most times it is not the change that is the problem but how the transitions are handled that is the problem.[ii] J.W. "Bill" Marriott, chairman and CEO of the international hotel and resort chain, says, "Take good care of your employees, and they'll take good care of your customers, and the customers will come back." [iii] So if you take care of your team of employees during the transition, your employees will take care of your customers and your customers will take care of your business. That is a win-win for everyone.

While I was preparing my speech I thought I might ask 1,700 of my friends on Facebook about change. Here are some of their remarks:

"Change is wonderful as long as everybody else does it."

"Change is here to stay."
"I love you, you're perfect, now change."

"I'm so broke that I can't afford to change my mind."

"Inflation is change."

"Change for the sake of change is not always a good thing; make sure the vision is a good vision first."

"The only thing worse than change is wishing you had."

Here's a thought: The Bible says that God doesn't change but it also says that God changes us. As we gaze at the Bible and Jesus, we are changed from the inside out. And when this life is over, we shall all be changed. Don't struggle against the changes that God makes. Learn to use them for your advantage!

Chapter 2

You Can Either Use Leadership or Be Used by Leadership

Leadership is not just a gift; it's a privilege. Leadership is for the benefit of others.

Everywhere I go in the world, I see leaders loved, hated, rising, falling, admired, ridiculed, celebrated or defeated. A leader in today's world can move from visible to invisible in a matter of days. Leadership is not just a gift; it's a privilege. Leadership is for the benefit of others. Leadership is not about ownership. Leadership is about stewardship, and the tricky part about leadership is the leader.

In *The 21 Indispensable Qualities of a Leader: Becoming the Person Others Will Want to Follow* (Thomas Nelson, 1999), author John Maxwell says that, above all other things, leadership is about the ability to influence. According to pollster George Barna, anyone can steer a ship, but it takes a real leader to chart the course. [iv] Warren Bennis writes in his book On Becoming a Leader that leadership is the ability to translate vision into reality. Stephen Covey notes, "The leader is the one who climbs the tallest tree, surveys the entire situation and yells, 'Wrong jungle!' " [v]

I was reading about good leadership recently. I found some ideas that I thought might be helpful to us all because we are all affected by leaders and leadership.

Here's the first thought: A good leader motivates, doesn't mislead, doesn't exploit. Good leaders are trustworthy. You can trust them, and that trust becomes motivational. It's a two-way relationship. As a follower, you are not a means to some leader's ego-driven end. Renowned anthropologist Margaret Mead is often quoted as saying, "What people say, what people do, and what they say they do are entirely different things." Trust is essential to leadership.

Good leaders abhor wrongdoing of all kinds; sound leadership has a moral foundation. In other words, as a leader, the first person you lead is you! Character determines long-term, sustainable success. British essayist and minister John Foster wrote, "A man without decision of character can never be said to belong to himself. He belongs to whatever can make captive of him." [vi]

Good leaders cultivate honest speech; they love advisors who tell them the truth. Good leaders listen to others even if it's not what they want to hear. Let me give you a humorous example called "Fore!":

My 5-year-old nephew wanted to caddy for my brother's golf game.

"You have to count my strokes," my brother told him. "How much is six plus nine plus eight?"

"Five," answered my nephew.

"Okay," my brother said, "let's go." [vii]

Enough said!

Good leaders invigorate lives; they are like spring rain and sunshine. Good leaders encourage us, rather than discourage us. They add to, rather than take from and that is a blessing. Leaders who build themselves up by tearing others down become depressing, discouraging and disturbing over time.

The mark of a good leader is loyal followers; leadership is nothing without a following. A good leader has loyal followers and a following. John Maxwell says, "If you get along, they'll go along." [viii] He also notes, "You've got to love your people more than your position." That doesn't mean they get everything they want. It means the leader is motivated by love, not ego or position.

Incidentally, the book where I found these leadership principles is a best seller and has been for years. It's called the Bible, and these good leadership thoughts come from Proverbs 16:10-15. You see, the Bible is relevant today too! The Bible — don't adjust it; trust it!

Chapter 3

Increasing Your Capacity and Competency in Times of Ambiguity

Hating people is like burning down your own house to get rid of a rat.
—Harry Emerson Fosdick, 20th Century Baptist and Presbyterian Minister

Recently I was in Jakarta, Indonesia, at a large conference called The Harvest Festival. The leader of the conference was Indonesian Pastor Jimmy Oentoro. Jimmy is the leader of more than 2,700 churches all over the world. He suggested to the 1,200 delegates that in dynamic times (times of ambiguity and change) we need to grow in key areas or we will be like someone making a credit-card call on a rotary dial phone — lost!

Once the world's richest man, J. Paul Getty wrote, "In times of rapid change, experience could be your worst enemy." [ix] According to William Boast, "Experience only helps in situations that have a degree of predictability; it is deadly in situations that require a fresh approach." [x] I would say these are changing times, wouldn't you?

Fortune magazine's September 23, 1991, issue ran a story on the minivan saying, "With over two million units sold, the [minivan] has been the mainstay of Chrysler profits since the mid-1980s." Its father, Hal Sperlich, first developed the idea at Ford but they wouldn't buy the idea. "'They lacked confidence that a market existed because the product didn't exist,' [Sperlich] says. … 'In ten years of developing the minivan we never once got a letter from a housewife asking us to invent one. To the skeptics, that proved there wasn't a market out there.' " [xi] The rest is history.

So in what areas did Pastor Oentoro challenge the delegates … and us … to grow? He used the concept of capacity. Increase your recognition capacity. Increase your faith capacity. Increase you vision capacity. Increase your leadership capacity. Increase your people capacity. Increase your change capacity. Increase your grace capacity. Increase your team capacity. Finally, increase your character capacity.

Let me start with talking about recognition capacity. Minivan father, Hal Sperlich, didn't just cognize minivans, he "re-cognized" the potential of minivans. He got an "ah-ha" on minivans. You rarely see what you are not looking for, and he was looking for it. He saw what Ford couldn't see and Chrysler did see. When opportunity wants to dance with you, you had better be on the dance floor.

Don't forget to increase your faith capacity when you recognize an opportunity. The Bible encourages us to grow in our faith, to enlarge our faith and to have an overcoming faith. Faith is doing something about what you recognize.

What is a vision? Pastor Terry Virgo calls it "a compelling picture of a preferable future that motivates us to perform." [xii] Sperlich had to have a vision or mental model of what a minivan would look like. He understood that everything is created first mentally, and then physically. He could see it and the future it held when others, significant others, couldn't. That is increasing your vision capacity.

Next, let's increase our leadership capacity. Do as John Maxwell suggested in Chapter 2, and chart your own course. Leadership moves us from dream to done. Faith is not the absence of doubt; faith is the presence of belief.

People and team capacity — now there's a difficult one for lots of folks. Many of us were reared with the one-man, hero-type of leadership that was prevalent years ago. The truth is that leaders today must view people as not merely pawns in some game, but as team members. John Maxwell states the following: "This is an irony: the more a leader gives his power away to others through encouragement, belief and resources to help them succeed, the more he gains power with them and assures his own success. You cannot give away love or power without gaining it in return." [xiii]

Maxwell goes on to say that in order for employees to feel empowered, they must have an opportunity to perform in an empowered way. They must have a sense of personal esteem. They must accept ownership of their job. They must feel they are part of the team. Finally, they must believe that they are a part of something significant. Jesus did that. He moved from the one-man, sage-on-the-stage type of leadership to the position of mentor in order to carry on the Father's business.

The idea of team is seen in the corporate offices of Walmart. "Through these doors pass ordinary people on their way to accomplishing extraordinary things." [xiv] I would say that about Jesus' disciples too. As John Maxwell's 2002 book title declares, "Teamwork makes the dream work!"

Now let's consider grace capacity. Most people are kind of like the license plate that states, "I'm OK ... You're So-So." That probably won't work too well today. Harry Emerson Fosdick said that hating people is like burning down your own house to get rid of a rat.[xv] Remember, grace recognizes consequences but refuses abandonment. I marvel at some of the things that Jesus endured in working with his team. For example, Peter denied Jesus three times during the most crucial part of His mission. Yet, Jesus didn't fire him or demote him. Jesus had grace capacity in essential areas of forgiveness and expectations. Yes, He did have boundaries but they were wide boundaries.

Finally, imagine growing in your character capacity. This is a challenging concept because today's society and the media continually blast messages about winning at any cost. Current thinking is that the end justifies the means. Today, when people have "moral high ground," they can do anything they want. That may get you where you want to be, but it won't keep you there. Sooner or later, what got you there won't keep you there. Character matters. There is a payday someday. And, whatever hits the fan will not be evenly distributed.

Increasing your knowledge, skills and awareness in today's world is mandatory if you want to thrive or even just survive in today's world. Change is here to stay. In fact change is such a constant that we are constantly changing. Usually, it's not the change that is the problem but how the transitions are handled inside of us that create the problem. Let's grow through this, not just go through this.

I love you, you're perfect, now change!

Chapter 4

Living High Relationship and High Task

High relationship/high task people finish the job well, build their marriage, team or country with people of opposing beliefs and, at the end of the day, can still get along.

A mother looked out a window and saw Bryson playing church with their three kittens. He had them lined up and was preaching to them. The mother turned around to do some work.

A while later she heard meowing and scratching on the door. She went to the window and saw Bryson, baptizing the kittens. She opened the door and said, "Bryson, stop that! You'll drown those kittens."

Bryson looked at her and said with much conviction in his voice: "They should have thought about that before they joined my church." [xvi]

Well, you might say that in this story, Bryson was really into task and not too much into relationship. Task was accomplished at the expense of relationship. We see that all the time. Someone wants to climb the corporate ladder and doesn't care what he or she has to do to get there. A politician wanting to win at all costs may adopt the "end justifies the means" philosophy and start building up himself by tearing down an opponent for the sake of the cause. Both leave the carnage of broken relationships and twisted truths on the side of the road.

Living life requires focus on both relationship and task. Adam and Eve were a great example of balanced relationship and task. "And God created man in His own image, in the image of God He created him; male and female He created them. And God blessed them; and God said to them, 'Be fruitful and multiply, and fill the earth, and subdue it; and rule over the fish of the sea and over the birds of the sky, and over every living thing that moves on the earth' " (Genesis 1:27-28).

God made male and female in order to be fruitful and multiply. Adam and Eve first learned about relationship. He gave the assignment of learning how to become "one flesh." They had to learn about agreement, unity and abundance. The two became one and the one became many. Out of their relationship came a family.

Then after relationship, God gave them a mission, or what I call task. God charged them with subduing and ruling the earth. He entrusted them with a task after their relationship was established. The two become one, the one became many, and the many do work, that is, accomplish tasks. Notice, relationship first, task second!

There are four ways of living life in terms of relationship/task. People or organizations may be high relationship/ low task. These people love everyone but achieve very little. Then there is the low relationship/ high task style of managing life. Task becomes everything and real relationships are obstacles that get in the way of what this type of person wants to accomplish. Relationships are conditional, requiring others to believe the way this person does. Third is the low relationship/low task style. This group dislikes or judges everyone and gets nowhere.

The final way of living is high relationship/high task. That's how Jesus lived. And many other successful people and organizations adopt this style. High relationship/high task people finish the job well, build their marriage, team or country with people of opposing beliefs and, at the end of the day, can still get along. Opposites can attract and then negotiate the differences if they understand the core value of relationships first. Many self-centered individuals and businesses and governments have lost that capacity in today's world.

Just think, right from the first days in the Bible, God was saying that teamwork makes the dream work. [xvii]

Chapter 5

Standing Out: Turning the Unusual Into the Usual

The first great gift we can bestow on others is a good example.
—Thomas Morell

The British newspaper, *The Times,* with typical tongue-in-cheek British wit, ran the following story about an unusual happenstance as though it were an ordinary occurrence:

"A young girl was blown out to sea on a set of inflatable teeth. She was rescued by a man on an inflatable lobster. A coastguard spokesman commented, 'This sort of thing is all too common.' " [xviii]

Isn't that interesting? As time goes by, what was uncommon becomes common. What was unusual becomes usual. What was once bizarre becomes commonplace. If you don't believe me, just look at women's fashions. As abnormal replaces normal, the abnormal becomes normal and then folks want the abnormal, which was once normal, again!

In these present times, it seems to me that people are getting tired of politics as usual, business as usual, media as usual, immorality as usual, and the like. The perversities of greed, power mongering, pandering, polarizing, and the end-justifies-the-means/win-at-all-costs approach have become accepted as normal. Maybe it's time to make what was once normal, which became abnormal, normal again! That's called wisdom. It takes more than someone on an inflatable lobster to run a country, city, business or university.

Let me give you an example of someone who stood out from the crowd of his time. You know of him. I'm referring to Abraham Lincoln before he was President of the United States.

The story is told of Lincoln that one day he watched a plantation owner bidding for a slave girl. Figuring he was going to buy her and abuse her, Lincoln paid the price to set her free. "Does this mean I can say whatever I want to say?" she asked. Lincoln replied, "Yes." Again she asked, "Does this mean I can go wherever I want to go?" Lincoln responded, "Yes, you're free!" With tears streaming down her face she replied, "Then sir, I will go with you." [xix]

Incidentally, that is a great picture of what Christ did for you and me. He paid the price for our freedom. Galatians 5:1 says, "It was for freedom that Christ set us free." Christ changed everything. He moved us from "we have to" to "we want to." That's unusual but that is what outstanding people do. Most don't even want to be recognized. They realize that, as 18th-century librettist Thomas Morell pointed out, the "first great gift we can bestow on others is a good example."

Let me close with this thought by William A. Ward:

"The more generous we are, the more joyous we become. The more cooperative we are, the more valuable we become. The more enthusiastic we are, the more productive we become. The more serving we are, the more prosperous we become. The more outgoing we are, the more helpful we become. The more curious we are, the more creative we become. The more patient we are, the more understanding we become. The more persistent we are, the more successful we become." [xx]

Now, you might ask, where are the people who stand out because they are outstanding? I know … and I see you! You are reading this chapter right now!

Chapter 6

The Balance Sheet of Life

What do you do after you make it to the top of your respective field and where do you go from there?

My friend Wilson Ng, a printer in Kuala Lumpur, Malaysia sent me a piece of Internet wisdom called "Balance Sheet of Life." [xxi] This is what it says:

> Our Birth is our Opening Balance.
> Our Death is our Closing Balance.
> Our Prejudiced Views are our Liabilities.
> Our Creative Ideas are our Assets.
> Heart is our Current Asset.
> Soul is our Fixed Asset.
> Brain is our Fixed Deposit.
> Thinking is our Current Account.
> Achievements are our Capital.
> Character & Morals, our Stock-in-Trade.
> Friends are our General Reserves.
> Values & Behavior are our Goodwill.

Patience is our Interest Earned.
Love is our Dividend.
Children are our Bonus Issues.
Education is Brands / Patents.
Knowledge is our Investment.
Experience is our Premium Account.
The Aim is to Tally the Balance Sheet of Life Accurately.
The Goal is to get the Best Presented Accounts Award.

I like that.

Last week I was a guest at a round-table discussion of eight very influential commerce leaders in Kuala Lumpur, Malaysia. I must tell you that I was stunned by these leaders' achievements and their success in their particular vocations. A former doctor, who is the group's moderator, asked me to present some ideas to these leaders by. This particular group had been meeting once a month for the last twelve years. Obviously, they are getting value from being there.

What struck me was that they had already reached the top in their respective fields in business, medicine, government, education and the like. I was told that one of the leaders even owned a significant part of a large town in Malaysia. What was I going to say to these people? What possible wisdom could I impart to these people of influence in places of influence in Malaysia?

The question I kept asking myself was, "What do you do after you make it to the top of your respective field and where do you go from there?"

The thought that I presented to them and now present to you is from physicist Albert Einstein. "Try become not a man of success, but try rather to become a man of value." [xxii] I challenged them to move beyond being a person of success to being a person of significance. Why not move from success financially to success socially and be the change?

In his book, *Giving Back: Discover Your Values and Put Them into Action Through Volunteering and Donating,* computer scientist Steven Ketchpel, calls leaders like these social entrepreneurs. "Social entrepreneurs address social problems with private sector strategies. Social entrepreneurs do what economic entrepreneurs do except in the social sector. They don't leave their business skills behind when they cross over to meeting social needs." [xxiii]

Mother Teresa was a person of significance. She was transformational. When she showed up, her presence shook people up. She was beyond reproach or accusation. She was small in stature but large in influence. She gave back! She understood that even with a healthy economy, a sick society may be sick.

Although not all people may reach the same degree of financial success, everyone can be significant socially.

Motivational speaker Zig Ziglar once said, "Where you start is not as important as where you finish." [xxiv] How's that Balance Sheet of Life looking?

Chapter 7

Ten Kinds of People I Wish We Could Help

In today's world a good scapegoat is nearly as welcome as a solution to the problem.
—Anonymous

"Hello Mrs. Frobisher," said the bearded guy behind the counter at the bagel shop. My husband and I looked at him but drew complete blanks. "I'm sorry, do we know each other?" I asked.
"Yeah, you was my English teacher."
Leaning over, my husband whispered, "Good job, Honey, good job." [xxv]

As they say, you can lead a horse to water but you can't make him drink. Recently, I was reading an article written by Pastor Joseph Mattera of Resurrection Church in New York City. He wrote about ten types of people he cannot help. Mattera explained that he had tried many times to help these ten types of people but, try as he may, he had learned the hard way that it just doesn't do any good.

Let me share with you the ten types of people he mentioned.

Number 1 Those who do not take responsibility for themselves.
Number 2 Those who do not have a heart to seek God.
Number 3 Those who create distance so that they are not accountable.
Number 4 Those who insist on a negative outlook on life.
Number 5 Those who refuse to have a vision for the future.
Number 6 Those who live in self-deception.
Number 7 Those who do not want to pay the price for success.
Number 8 Those whose primary agenda is individualistic.
Number 9 Those who do not keep covenant or keep promises.
Number 10 Those who lack transparency, humility and integrity. [xxvi]

Does this list seem kind of scary to you? If you are like most every other human being, you are thinking of people you know who have some of those characteristics. Come on now, I know you were thinking about others, weren't you? We all do that. But let's stop thinking about others for a moment and consider yourself. Have some of these tendencies consistently become attitudes or behaviors in your life? Could you be one of these types of people, and that is why rain keeps falling on your head? I'm not pointing my finger at anyone. I'm just asking all of us to consider and ask ourselves if we have knowingly or unknowingly slipped into one of these ten categories. Someone once observed that in today's world a good scapegoat is nearly as welcome as a solution to the problem. Another person said that nothing stinks more than that moment during an argument when you realize you're wrong. Perhaps a little truth encounter would do us all some good and get us unstuck.

H. Jackson Brown, Jr., bestselling author of *A Father's Book of Wisdom* and *Life's Little Instruction Book* wrote, "Talent without discipline is like an octopus on roller skates. There's plenty of movement, but you never know if it's going to be forward, backwards or sideways."

Perhaps a little wisdom by Mark Twain might help: "The only way to keep your health is to eat what you don't want, drink what you don't like and do what you'd rather not." Sometimes we have to give up to go up and that often comes by our choice and God's great willingness and availability to help.

Chapter 8

The Sage on the Stage or the Guide by Their Side?

Thank God for the people of significance and value, the unsung heroes who support but don't get the accolades.

There was a farmer who collected horses and he only needed one more breed to complete his collection. One day, he found out that his neighbor had the particular breed of horse that he needed. The motivated farmer bothered his neighbor until he sold the horse to him.

A month later, the horse became ill. The farmer called his veterinarian who said, "Your horse has a virus. He must take this medicine for three days. I'll come back on the third day and if he's not better, we're going to have to put him down."

Nearby, the pig listened closely to their conversation. The farmer gave the horse the medicine. The pig approached the horse and said, "Be strong, my friend. Get up or else they're going to put you to sleep!"

On the second day, the farmer gave the horse the medicine again. The pig approached the horse and said, "Come on buddy, get up or else you're going to die! Come on, I'll help you get up. Let's go! One, two, and three ... now get up!" But the horse did not respond.

On the third day, the medicine was administered again. The veterinarian then said to the farmer, "Unfortunately, we're going to have to put your horse down tomorrow. Otherwise, the virus he has might spread and infect the other horses."

After they left, the pig approached the horse. "Listen pal, it's now or never! Get up! Come on! Have courage! Come on! Get up! Get up! That's it, slowly! Great! Come on, one, two, and three! Good, good! Now faster, come on. Fantastic! Run! Run more! Yes! You did it!"

When the farmer came back and saw the horse running in the field, he began shouting, "It's a miracle! My horse is cured! This deserves a party. Let's kill the pig!" [xxvii]

Have you ever felt like that pig? You worked really hard in a supporting role to accomplish a goal, and when success finally came along, your boss got all the credit. Or perhaps you invented something working for your company, but your company got the patent. Then you got fired because you weren't needed anymore. Who gets the accolades, the quarterback or the offensive line?

Learning to live without recognition is truly a humbling experience. Our culture focuses on the "sage on the stage" rather than the "guide by their side." But, as you and I should know, not much happens without the contributors who make things happen.

Thank God for the people of significance and value, the unsung heroes who support but don't get the accolades. My wife Becky is a perfect example. As pastor and speaker, I get accolades. She has the hard job. She puts up with me. The truth is I may be the flame-thrower but God and Becky are the fuel.

Here is a word of encouragement for you "guides by their side." Jesus said in the Beatitudes, "Blessed are the gentle or humble, for they shall inherit the earth" (Matthew 5:5). In other words, the crowd may not know who did the work, but God does. Wait until you see who gets the accolades in heaven!

Chapter 9

Two Contrasting Styles of Leadership, Both Called EGO

Jesus demonstrated EGO leadership — Exalt God Only — instead of human EGO — Edging God Out.

Everywhere I travel these days I find people who are upset with the current leadership in government, business, education, and pretty much every other area where relationships are involved. It's like flies on a screen door. The flies on the inside want out and the flies on the outside want in. People are swinging from one extreme to another extreme looking for a leader whom they can trust, who is honest and not self-serving. Most people sense that something is wrong. But identifying what's wrong is a much harder issue.

Dr. Loren Gresham, president of Southern Nazarene University, observed, "True leadership must be for the benefit of the people, not just the enrichment of the institution."[xxviii] I might add not just for the sake of philosophy or political position.

As I noted earlier, Stephen Covey describes a leader as one who climbs the tallest tree, surveys the situation and yells, "Wrong jungle!" The story is told in Matthew 20:20-28 of a time Jesus yelled, "wrong jungle" to some of His leadership. The mother of two of His leaders, James and John, came to Jesus and tried to manipulate Him into giving them the highest places of honor, sitting on Jesus' right and left side, in His kingdom to come. This got all the other leaders thoroughly disgusted at both the sons and the mother. Perhaps this kind of thing is what gets so many people disgusted and frustrated with leaders in today's world too.

Look at what Jesus says to the other disgruntled leaders about true leadership: "You've observed how godless rulers throw their weight around, how quickly a little power goes to their heads. It's not going to be that way with you. Whoever wants to be great must become a servant. Whoever wants to be first among you must be your servant. That is what the Son of Man has done; He came to serve, not be served" (Matthew 20:23-25 Message).

Jesus used this incident to define real leadership, the kind of leadership that is not EGO-driven but EGO-driven. In his book *Lead Like Jesus*, Ken Blanchard writes that human leadership must not elbow its way to the front or take over. Ego-centered, ego-prominent humanistic leadership betrays the type of leadership God wants. According to Blanchard, Jesus demonstrated EGO leadership ... "Exalt God Only" ... instead of human EGO ... "Edging God Out." [xxix]

It doesn't matter which political party or side of an argument we are affiliated with. What frustrates people is ego-driven, ego-centered leaders who plunder the people they are leading. We see this type of leadership style in every setting in which there is a leader. It could be in a marriage, a company, a school, a church, a city or a nation.

The Edging God Out style always creates separation from God, from others and within us. It creates comparison, classification and commendation. It distorts the truth into a false sense of security — an us vs. them/win-lose/right-wrong type of mindset that ultimately divides a house against itself. It thrives on instant gratification, recognition, power, and being the center of attention. Does that sound familiar?

Maybe it is time to stop complaining and start serving, voting for, marrying, working for, following, and being a leader who puts aside the EGO that Edges God Out and uses the EGO that Exalts God Only. Ah ha!

Chapter 10

Unique Realistic Perspectives on Leadership

Timing is as important as what to do and where to go.

A few weeks ago, a graduating university student asked me five questions on leadership for a paper he was writing. I tried to think outside of the box in answering these questions. I thought that what I shared with him might be helpful to you. His questions and my answers follow:

What makes a good leader? John Maxwell says a good leader needs the convictions to keep focused, the creativity to keep relevant, the foundation to keep him/her solid, and the vision or faith to keep soaring. Also, an effective leader has to be able to endure pain.[xxx] A leader said it this way: "My level of leadership is based on my willingness to endure pain in making difficult decisions." One pastor said that every time your church attendance doubles, fifty percent of your staff can't go with you. Whether in business or church leadership, people will come and go. Many can't endure that kind of pain and yet effective leadership requires it.

How have you grown as a leader over your lifetime? I have come to understand timing. Timing is as important as what to do and where to go. You can have the best idea ever but if it is released too soon or too late, the great idea will look like a bad idea. Alfred Sloan once said, "Success does not lie in your ability to adjust to change. Success lies in your ability to anticipate change." [xxxi] In these dynamic changing times, success will happen for those who know the times and what to do, who to do it with, how to do it, and when to do it.

How important is character in leadership? As someone once said, "Vision will grow a business but character sustains it." Character determines success. One of the biggest character issues that I see in many leaders is using people as a means to their own end. Many leaders these days are searching for significance, and the size of their ministry or business is their source of significance. Successful leaders have learned how to live from significance rather than for significance. In other words, a leader cannot lead people if he or she needs people. Leaders who need the adulation of people, who use people to feel good about themselves disqualify themselves from objective decision making.

What would be your advice to me as to how I can grow as a leader? Understand that there are paradoxes in leadership. A good leader knows what to do in the season that you need to do it in. For example, knowing there are times when a leader must serve (Matthew 20:25-28), as well as times when a leader must rule (I Timothy 5:17). A leader must be confident (Matthew 7:29) as well as humble (James 4:10). A leader must be a person of action (Gospel of Mark) as well as a person of prayer (Luke 18:1). A leader must have a strategy (Luke 14:28-32) as well as a willingness to submit to God's will (Acts 16:1-10). Knowing when to be what is leadership in action.

What should I avoid to be a good leader? Letting the fact that you are a leader go to your head. Pride precedes the fall. Also, the more a leader empowers, the more that leader gains power. The converse is true also. Finally, become a person of significance rather than a person of success. Mother Teresa was a person of significance. Many leaders pursue success rather than significance to both their detriment and their community's detriment. Conquest without contribution hurts everyone.

Chapter 11

When a Wright Was Wrong

It takes 10 hands to score a basket.
— Former UCLA Basketball Coach John Wooden

In the latter part of the nineteenth century, when the Methodist church was holding its denominational convention, one leader stood up and shared his vision both for the church and for society at large. He told the ministers and evangelists how he believed someday men would fly from place to place instead of merely traveling on horseback. But it was a concept too outlandish for many members to handle.

One minister, Bishop Wright, stood up and angrily protested. "Heresy!" he shouted. "Flight is reserved for the angels!" He went on to elaborate that if God had intended for man to fly, He would have given him wings. Clearly, the bishop was unable to envision what the speaker was predicting. When Bishop Wright finished his brief protest, he gathered up his two sons, Orville and Wilbur, and left the auditorium.

That's right. Bishop Wright's sons were Orville and Wilbur Wright. Several years later, on December 17, 1903, those two sons did what their father called impossible. They made "the first free, controlled, and sustained flights in a power-driven, heavier-than-air machine" that day. [xxxii] Of those four flights, the first lasted only 12 seconds, but the fourth lasted 59 seconds and took them 852 feet. The two brothers partnered together to accomplish the impossible — and in the process, they changed the world. They discovered the power of partnership. [xxxiii]

I found that story in John Maxwell and Tim Elmore's book *The Power of Partnership in the Church.* Here is their definition of partnership: "Partnership is the ability to work together toward a common vision. It is the ability to direct individual accomplishment toward organized objectives. It is the fuel that allows common people to attain uncommon results. Simply put, it is less 'me' and more 'we.' " That's a great definition for success when you're at your wit's end.

It takes uncommon sense to navigate seas of crisis. You discover wisdom and strength when you find a partner, spouse or a good friend. Most times you get more than a facelift, you get a "faith" lift! The Bible points this out in Psalm 133:1. "Behold, how good and how pleasant it is for brothers to dwell together in unity!" Notice the words "dwell together." Andrew Carnegie said, "It marks a big step in your development when you realize that other people can help you do a better job than you could do alone." [xxxiv] Basketball coach John Wooden said, "It takes 10 hands to score a basket." [xxxv]

Former University of Colorado football coach and founder of Promise Keepers Bill McCartney once said, "We have not come together to compete with one another, but to complete one another." A.W. Tozer said, "God is looking for people through whom He can do the impossible — what a pity that we plan only the things we can do by ourselves."[xxxvi] None of us is as smart as all of us.

Still doubting? Just ask Orville and Wilbur Wright — who were right!

Chapter 12

When Progress Is Progress

The more our culture changes and progresses, the more we need to progress in wisdom to ensure that we don't create more problems than we solve.

If you are tired of your children complaining about life in today's world, look at these statistics about the United States in 1906. What a difference a century makes!

The average life expectancy was 47 years. Only 14 percent of the homes at that time had a bathtub. Only eight percent of the homes had a telephone. A three-minute call from Denver to New York City cost 11 dollars. There were only 8,000 cars and only 144 miles of paved roads. The maximum speed limit in most cities was 10 miles per hour. Alabama, Mississippi, Iowa and Tennessee were more heavily populated than California. With a mere 1.4 million people, California was only the twenty-first most populous state in the Union.

The tallest structure in the world was the Eiffel Tower. The average wage was 22 cents per hour. The average worker made between $200 and $400 per year. A competent accountant could expect to earn $2,000 per year, a dentist $2,500 per year, a veterinarian between $1,500 and $4,000 per year and a mechanical engineer about $5,000 per year. More than 95 percent of all births took place at home. Ninety percent of all medical doctors had no college education. Instead, they attended so-called medical schools, many of which were condemned by the press and the government as "substandard."

The cost of sugar was 4 cents a pound, eggs were 14 cents per dozen and coffee was 15 cents a pound. Most women washed their hair only once a month and used borax or egg yolks for shampoo. The five leading causes of death were pneumonia and influenza, tuberculosis, diarrhea, heart disease and stroke. The American flag had 45 stars. The population of Las Vegas, Nevada, was 30. Crossword puzzles, canned beer and ice tea hadn't even been invented yet. Two out of every three U. S. adults couldn't read or write and only 6 percent had graduated from high school. There were only 230 reported murders in the entire USA.

As they used to say in those commercials, "You've come a long way, baby!" Now, think about this: Imagine what the USA and the world will be like in another 100 years. Frightening, isn't it? Yet this is what the prophet Daniel predicted in the Bible a long, long time ago. And the Lord told him, "This is a confidential report, Daniel, for your eyes and ears only. Keep it secret. Put the book under lock and key until the end. In the interim there is going to be a lot of frantic running around, trying to figure out what's going on" (Message).

My take on this is that the more our culture changes and progresses, the more we need to progress in wisdom to ensure that we don't create more problems than we solve. Progress isn't necessarily progress unless we are progressing in all areas, not just in our technology. We need to progress just as much in wisdom as in knowledge.[xxxvii] We will need the convictions to keep focused, the creativity to keep us relevant, the foundation to keep us solid and the faith to keep us soaring.

We get that foundational part and that faith part from God. If we forget God and replace Him with technology, the sound of our own wheels will drive us crazy!

Chapter 13

Acknowledging the Reality but Seeing the Remedy

Admiral Nimitz was able to see the big picture and find the silver lining in a situation where everyone else could see only doom and gloom.

December 7, 2011, marked the 70th anniversary of the bombing of Pearl Harbor. In William H. Ewing's book *Nimitz: Reflections on Pearl Harbor,* the author cites U.S. Fleet Admiral Chester W. Nimitz's recollections about this turbulent period in world history. Ewing describes how Nimitz put a positive spin on one of America's worst military disasters following the admiral's assignment to take over command of the Pacific fleet.

Admiral Nimitz flew to Hawaii to assume command of the Pacific Fleet, landing at Pearl Harbor on Christmas Eve 1941. There was such a spirit of despair, dejection and defeat. On Christmas Day 1941, Nimitz was given a boat tour of the destruction wrought on Pearl Harbor. Big sunken battleships and navy vessels cluttered the waters everywhere he looked.

As the tour boat returned to dock, the young helmsman of the boat asked, "Well Admiral, what do you think after seeing all this destruction?"

To the shock of everyone within the sound of his voice, Admiral Nimitz replied, "The Japanese made three of the biggest mistakes an attack force could ever make, or God was taking care of America. Which do you think it was?"

Surprised, the young helmsman asked, "What do mean by saying the Japanese made the three biggest mistakes an attack force ever made?" Nimitz continued with his explanation. Mistake number one was that the Japanese attacked on Sunday morning. Nine out of every ten crewmen of those ships were ashore on leave. If those same ships had been lured to sea and been sunk, there would have been 38,000 men lost instead of 3,800.

Nimitz recalled mistake number two. "When the Japanese saw all those battleships lined in a row, they got so carried away sinking those battleships, they never once bombed the dry docks opposite those ships. If they had destroyed the dry docks, we would have had to tow every one of those ships to America to be repaired. As it is now, the ships are in shallow water and can be raised. One tug can pull them over to the dry docks, and we can have them repaired and at sea by the time we could have towed them to America. And I already have crews ashore anxious to man those ships."

Nimitz concluded with mistake number three. "Every drop of fuel in the Pacific theater of war is in ground storage tanks five miles away over that hill. One attack plane could have strafed those tanks and destroyed our fuel supply. That's why I say the Japanese made three of the biggest mistakes an attack force could make, or God was taking care of America." [xxxviii]

Now please don't think that I'm bashing the Japanese or something like that. I have spoken in Japan many, many times. The Japanese are wonderful people but from time to time, like most nations, they have inherited adversarial and destructive leadership. Such was the time then. I want to emphasize how Admiral Nimitz was able to see the big picture and find the silver lining in a situation where everyone else could see only doom and gloom. He gave all those present an earthly and heavenly perspective that none of them had ever considered. America needed a leader like that.

True leadership acknowledges the reality but sees the remedy. Real leaders also understand that in the darkest hour lies God greatest power.

Chapter 14

A Wiser Way to Look for a Leader or Candidate

Why couldn't all the king's horses and all the king's men put Humpty Dumpty back together again? Perhaps it's because they didn't ask the King!

Let's start with a story called "Military Inspection":

The colonel who served as inspector general in our command paid particular attention to how personnel wore their uniforms. On one occasion he spotted a junior airman with a violation.

"Airman," he bellowed, "what do you do when a shirt pocket is unbuttoned?"

The startled airman replied, "Button it, sir!"

The colonel looked him in the eye and said, "Well?"

At that, the airman nervously reached over and buttoned the colonel's shirt pocket. [xxxix]

A good example is far better than a good precept, isn't it?

In these days when we are being bombarded with so many problems in nations, finances, and governments, I thought it might be beneficial to investigate what God looks for in a leader and what kind of leader God endorses for a nation, city or precinct.

In my opinion, if there is one verse in the Bible that summarizes effective government leadership, it is I Chronicles 14:2. "And David realized that the Lord had established him as king over Israel, and that his kingdom was highly exalted, for the sake of His people Israel."

In this verse I see two reasons why God chose David to be the leader of a nation. First, David had the humility to understand that God put him in a leadership position of great authority. But secondly, he also realized that with privilege comes responsibility. He was exalted to his royal throne for the sake of God's people. He realized he was a steward, not the owner of the nation.

The Bible says that there is no authority except from God, and those that exist are established by God (Romans 13:1). The Bible also says that the king's heart is like channels of water in the hand of the Lord, He turns it wherever He wishes (Proverbs 21:1). It takes humility to acknowledge that. David really "got it." God granted him leadership for all the people in his constituency, not for just a loud outspoken few. Why? God loves everyone, and a good leader must have the bigger picture in mind.

All political candidates, and especially those who serve as "kings" (that is, in governing positions of authority over members of the citizenry), should come to the understanding that the position they were elected to and serve in is for others, not for their own benefit. For example, if they are elected mayor, they must realize the fact that the city does not exist on their behalf; they are there for the city. A mayor must not use the city as a means to his or her ego-driven end or agenda.

Let me ask you a question. Why couldn't all the king's horses and all the king's men put Humpty Dumpty back together again? Perhaps it's because they didn't ask the King! Let's get a little wisdom from the King on putting our communities, cities and nation back together again.

Maybe it's time to start looking for leaders with David's humility and understanding of stewardship. Personally, I'm tired of emotionally manipulative popularity contests based on who has raised the most money to run negative commercials against the other candidate. Throwing mud is just losing ground. It's not good leadership either.

Chapter 15

Nothing In Life Is More Important Than Believability!

Adam blamed Eve, Eve blamed the snake and the snake didn't have a leg to stand on!

A minister told his congregation, "Next week I plan to speak about the sin of lying. To help you understand my sermon, I want you all to read chapter 17 in the gospel of Mark.

The following Sunday, as he prepared to deliver his sermon, the minister asked for a show of hands. He wanted to know how many had read Mark 17. Almost every hand went up. The minister smiled and said, "Mark has only 16 chapters. I will now proceed with my sermon on the sin of lying." [xl]

When God gives us His wisdom, it's always for our own good. What He calls sin or "missing God's mark," is not meant to condemn us but to help us. Sin is hurtful not because it is forbidden; it is forbidden because it is hurtful. This is true in the case of lying. God's admonition in the Ten Commandments is to be truthful. Why? Because lying and deception are the number one cause of breakdowns in relationships. Relationship requires trust. Making commitments generates hope. Keeping commitments generates trust. In other words, lying destroys trust, and trust is the currency of relationships. Trust connects you to that person or institution.

Lying started back in the Garden of Eden. The serpent that tempted Eve in the garden was an expert at half-truths and deceit. He could make a mountain out of a molehill. He had more verbal twists and turns than a tornado. He was convincing and, just in case, he could make a case where there was no case. Adam and Eve fell for the spin. Eat this apple and you will be like God, knowing good and evil. In other words, you will be the judge of everything, king of the world and one with privilege but no responsibility.

Well, you know the story; Adam and Eve fell for the lie and started lying themselves. They produced what they fell for. When the Lord God came to find out what was going on, Adam blamed Eve, Eve blamed the snake and the snake didn't have a leg to stand on! Was God trying to stop Adam and Eve from having fun? No way! God was trying to save their relationship. God was trying to keep their trust intact. The result is that men and women have had strained relationships from that day forward.

Adam and Eve's blame shift was really just a "shame shift." They fell, they hid, they got angry, and they got fearful. The facts were overlooked and the end-justifies-the-means strategy of coping came into existence. They had to look perfect, to be large and in charge, and the truth was suppressed by lying and fabrication. Authenticity and integrity were replaced by expedience. Expedience is doing whatever you have to do in order for you and the cause you're pushing to look good. But the worst thing about being deceived is that you are deceived!

Where did all that start? A lie that created fear that produced a lifestyle and culture wherein lying and half-truths are acceptable and expected. No wonder relationships are at an all-time low. No one believes anyone very much any more.

If you tell the truth the first time, you will never have to try and remember what you said. That's good advice.

Jesus was always truthful. His integrity intimidated lawyers, politicians and hypocrites. They reacted to His honesty. Honesty is a force. Wouldn't it be wonderful, in this day and age, if we all could be less political? Much of the time, politics — especially national politics — is the art of making one's own selfish interest seem like the national interest, then using any means necessary to profit those interests.

What if we were like the person in Psalm 15:4 who walked in integrity and always told the truth even if it was to his own hurt? I'll bet that person would have many strong relationships because he could be trusted to at least tell the truth. Such integrity would work for him, not against him, in the eyes of God and other people. After all, the wonderful thing about being wrong is the joy that it brings to others. It certainly is much better to be true-faced than two-faced.

Chapter 16

A Real Life Lesson for Madeleine that Made a Mother's Day!

Don't just spend time with your children; invest time with your children too.

Like you, I have several different labels by which people may know me. You might know me as a columnist, an author, a speaker, a father, or maybe a pastor. But, to my 5-year-old granddaughter Madeleine, I'm "Oupa." That name carries all kinds of responsibilities with it. I have to be funny, spend time with her, bring her a treat, and chase after her. I do that for my two other granddaughters, too.

Let me share with you a life lesson that my daughter (Madeleine's mother) recently sent me. If you are a parent, an Oupa, a Nana, or want to be any of these in the future, you might want to pay attention to my daughter's story. Read on.

"So … I have to tell you about a little Madeleine adventure. Yesterday, Madeleine, Tessa (Madeleine's little sister) and I went to a department store. "Madeleine saw a stuffed Clifford (the big red dog) and, of course, wanted it instantly. Well, you, Oupa, have seen the mountain of stuffed animals that she has and doesn't use anymore. However, she wanted a Clifford so here is the deal we made.

"Her Daddy and I were not going to buy the Clifford for her, but what she could do was go through her stuffed animals and pick out the ones she doesn't play with anymore. Since we were going to have a yard sale soon, she could have her own table and sell her stuffed animals to make the money to buy Clifford.

"She did a great job! She asked people if they wanted to buy a stuffed animal. On her own, she walked up to one lady and asked, 'Would you like to buy a stuffed animal for your child? We have one for boys.' She said that because most of her stuffed animals were pink or more girl-looking. She would take their money and say, 'Thank you.' When I prompted her she would even say, 'Have a nice day.'

"When no one was at our home during the garage sale, she would lament. But as soon as a car drove into the cul-de-sac she would shriek, 'Look Mama … a CUSTOMER!'

Madeleine made enough money to buy the Clifford she wanted and even had extra to buy a Cleo — Clifford's purple doggie pal. A couple of people even made a dollar-or-two donation to the Clifford fund after hearing the story, but most of her money was due to sales. (And being as cute as a button didn't hurt either — Oupa's note.)

"This was a great lesson for Madeleine. It was great to see her come out of her shell a bit. Clifford was big motivation. We are very proud of our girl." [xli]

I know that many parents are busy these days with work, life and trying to stay ahead. But remember that just a few special things, like my daughter did for Madeleine, can go a long way in developing the character, initiative, and responsibility that children will need when they grow up. Don't just spend time with your children; invest time with your children too.

Happy Mother's Day!

Chapter 17

Finding and Keeping a Job in Challenging Times

***You will only be remembered for two things: the problems you solve or the problems you create.* —Mike Murdock**

The Bible is relevant and speaks of heaps of characters applying for jobs as well as keeping jobs in crisis times. After all, finding a job and keeping a job are two different issues.

To find a good job when there are few good jobs around is like trying out for a sports team. You need to stand out by becoming outstanding. You need to separate yourself from the rest of the field. You have to create a climate of acceptance, influence and favor. Joseph did that with Pharaoh, Daniel did that with Nebuchadnezzar, and Esther did that with King Ahasuerus. So, how do you do that? Let me give you four suggestions.

Mike Murdock calls this first suggestion the Power of Appearance.[xlii] The Bible says that man looks at the outward appearance (I Samuel 16:7). The way you dress and groom sends a message to others. Genesis 41:14 tells us that when Joseph wanted a job serving the ruler of Egypt, "he shaved himself, and changed his clothes, and came to Pharaoh." He changed his appearance to create favor with the King.

Light travels faster than sound. People see what you are before they hear what you are. The vice president of a major employment agency once said that the hiring of 90 percent of employees is based mainly on their physical appearance alone. Even if you can't afford expensive clothes, you can be clean. Appearance could be the determining factor in getting a good job.

Next is the Power of Aptitude. Become the best you can be in the field you desire. The Bible says, "Observe people who are good at their work. Skilled workers are always in demand and admired; they don't take a back seat to anyone" (Proverbs 22:29). It has been estimated that 84 percent of workers demand constant supervision to assure completion of their tasks and work. Another 14 percent must have some supervision. Only two percent of the workers of America will work and complete their tasks and responsibilities without any supervision. They are the highest paid and first hired.

Now, consider the Power of Attitude. Mike Murdock says, "You will only be remembered for two things: the problems you solve or the problems you create. Your attitude toward life, your work and people can cause you to rise to the top of your company or stay where you are." Attitude is your best friend or your worst enemy.

Here are some biblical principles designed to empower you to stand out. Learn to control your anger. Don't make weak excuses when you resent doing something you have been asked to do. Don't become a complainer or a gossip on your job. Don't flatter others to get ahead. Give sincere praise and encouragement when appropriate. Be honest about your mistakes. Don't be a time thief. Don't spread rumors.

Lastly, consider the Power of Atmosphere. Your state of mind determines your behavior. That atmosphere attracts or repels others. Learn to improve the atmosphere around you by creating an atmosphere of integrity, peace and stability. God can make that happen if you will cooperate. Many times the things that come to those who wait will be the things left by those who got there first. Improve, don't pollute, the atmosphere of everyone around you.

Sometimes life is like your medicine bottle that reads, "Shake well before using." Sometimes God has to do that with people. He shakes them well so they will be usable again. I'm also aware that many of you know and apply these principles and you lost your job anyway. If that is you, hang in there. Ninety-year-old columnist Regina Brett says, "Whatever doesn't kill you really does make you stronger." [xliii]

Chapter 18

Getting In and Out of the Trap of Disappointment

It is not a matter of if, but when, people, leaders, products, institutions, and a multitude of other circumstances will disappoint us.

Here is a story I received in my e-mail. I think it holds some real wisdom for us.

A professor in a large university and an exchange student had an interesting discussion one day. The student asked a strange question to the professor. "Do you know how to catch wild pigs?" The professor thought it was a joke.

"You catch wild pigs by finding a suitable place in the woods and putting corn on the ground. The pigs find it and begin to come every day to eat the free corn. When they are used to coming every day, you put a fence down one side of the place where they are used to coming. When they get used to the fence, they begin to eat the corn again and you put up another side of the fence."

The exchange student went on. "They get used to that and start to eat again. You continue until you have all four sides of the fence up with a gate in the last side. The pigs, which are used to the free corn, start to come through the gate to eat that free corn again. You then slam the gate on them and catch the whole herd. Suddenly the wild pigs have lost their freedom. They run around and around inside the fence, but they are caught. Soon they go back to eating the free corn. They are so used to it that they have forgotten how to forage in the woods for themselves, so they accept their captivity." [xliv]

I'm not sure if that is a true story but it sure makes sense to me. And, one thing is for certain — it is easier not to get into a trap than it is to get out of a trap.

I would like to address the subject of disappointment in relation to this story. We have all been disappointed from time to time. Jesus said that this would happen. He said in Matthew 11 and 18 that it is inevitable that stumbling blocks will come in this life. It is not a matter of if, but when, people, leaders, products, institutions, and a multitude of other circumstances will disappoint us.

Pastor Alan Pateman notes that it is all too easy to give in to the "feelings" of disappointment, mainly where other people or leaders are involved. "I have learned to get over disappointment as quickly as possible; the alternative is for unforgiveness to set in, which only taints our inner focus (spiritual sight), rendering us unavailable to be used by God any longer."[xlv] That is a good thought.

The longer one stays in the clutches of disappointment, the more one can be trapped like those wild pigs. Disappointment held over a period of time can turn into dissatisfaction, displeasure, distress, discontent, disenchantment, disillusionment, frustration or regret. Disappointment is also free. Get the message?

Here is some wisdom. Get a real perspective on your disappointment. Let's choose to stay out of that trap. The real person it hurts is you. Your will and God's power are more than enough to overcome deep-seated disappointment.

Chapter 19

Fostering Defining Moments in Young Leaders' Lives

People occasionally stumble and make mistakes, sometimes really big mistakes. There is no such thing as perfect people or a perfect business.

Here is an interesting story that occurred some years ago.

An executive secretary to the president of a large corporation made a costly mistake, which cost the company $50,000. She was devastated and brought her letter of resignation to the president explaining, "I realize what a dumb thing I did. I am very sorry. I know that it cost the company $50,000. Here is my letter of resignation."

"Are you crazy?" her boss thundered. "I have been teaching you and educating you every week. Now, you have made a big mistake. I have just invested $50,000 in your education and you're going to leave? No, ma'am. You are not going to leave. You have cost me too much to lose my investment in you." She stayed and became an extraordinary executive.[xlvi]

As they say, failure is a teacher, not an undertaker. L. Thomas Holdcroft once said, “The past is a guidepost, not a hitching post.” [xlvii] As another saying goes, “Age is an awfully high price to pay for maturity.”

I love the response of the woman in this story. She chose to be teachable, not offended or defensive. She took responsibility. She grew through the problem and didn’t repeat it. She followed the counsel of James 4:10 and humbled herself, and then received promotion. Her humility and willingness to take responsibility took her to the top. She expected the worst then received the best.

But it takes two to make this work. Notice the president in this article. This man wasn’t condescending, petty or critical. Mary Kay Ash, the hugely successful founder of Mary Kay Cosmetics, once said, “Criticize the act, not the person.”

This president realized that people occasionally stumble and make mistakes, sometimes really big mistakes. There is no such thing as perfect people or a perfect business. As a business leader, he realized that people are in the process of growing and learning. This mentor allowed his student to learn, which allowed her to grow in turn. It takes a real leader to do that.

The president accepted the responsibility for the mistakes of those under his authority. He understood that with privilege comes responsibility. As a result, he was able to foster a defining moment in a young executive’s life. He realized that this particular woman would grow through this, not just go through this incident. I wish every mentor and students worked together that way.

Jesus accepted responsibility for those under Him, too. When Peter denied the Lord, Jesus prayed for him. Later, when Peter cut off the ear of the high priest's slave, Jesus healed the slave. Jesus, in effect was saying, Peter you are going to learn from these experiences and grow. Peter grew and helped change the world.

I realize that some mistakes can be deadly, but most aren't. Can't we act a little more like this president? Forgiveness makes the future possible, and great leaders accept responsibility for their troops! Jesus was our supreme example of this. His heart of compassion acted on the behalf of another. The investment was high but the returns were, and continue to be, higher.

Chapter 20

Impatient Journeys of the Earth Kind

Sometimes the only thing worse than waiting is wishing you had.

Someone once said, "Time may be a great healer, but it's a lousy beautician!" Let's explore one of God's ways called patience or long-suffering. I want to look at God's patience with us and our patience with God and with others. I want us to learn how to give time time, or, better said, to give God time. After all, to God, one day is as a thousand years and a thousand years as one day (2 Peter 3:8).

One of the fruits of the Spirit is patience. The first thing God says about love is that it is patient. When you get married, you don't get a marriage license, you get a patience license! How? With your spouse, your children and yourself! Ah ha!

God bears with us for many years, as does your spouse (I couldn't resist that!) God was patient with Adam and Eve, patient with Abram and Sarah, patient with Moses … about 40 years' worth, and patient with the Apostle Paul … about 40 years, too. God waited more than 30 years before His very own Son started His ministry. Jesus showed incredible patience with His new "board of directors" — from impulsive Peter to doubtful Thomas. Israel was in captivity 70 years in Babylon waiting for God's timing. God's favorite song is "Time is on my Side." Oh, yes it is! Farmers have to be patient, shepherds shepherding sheep have to be patient, fishermen need patience, building a church or business takes patience, battling stubborn enemies requires patience, and driving on freeways takes patience! Talk about God's patience with us, just look at the story of the prodigal son.

There is a cost to impatience. When Moses was receiving the Ten Commandments up on the mountain, the sons of Israel became impatient and built a gold calf in the valley. The cost of their impatience was devastating. Remember the man who said to Elisha, "Why should I wait for God?" He got "trampled underfoot by man" (2 Kings 7:17). Man didn't trample him; impatience trampled him. Just like the children of Israel in their long journey to freedom, we can become impatient because of the journey.

Are you or I impatient because of the journey? The Bible notes, "They quickly forgot His works and did not wait for His counsel" (Psalm 106:13). Sometimes the only thing worse than waiting is wishing you had. Believe me, you don't want God to work fast in most cases — you just might be the recipient of it!

There are impatient journeys that can really set us back if we don't know how to handle them. We can be impatient with God, our spouse or our family. Many have called their brothers and sisters "bothers and sinisters." We can be impatient with others, our careers, bosses, our country and even ourselves.

When my daughter Kristin was growing up, we used to sing a song together. It went like this: “Have patience, have patience, don’t be in such a hurry. When you get impatient, you only start to worry. Remember, remember, that God is patient too, and think of all the times when others have to wait for you.” [xlviii] Good advice!

The Bible says that patience of spirit is better than haughtiness of spirit (Ecclesiastes 7:8). We are to be patient when wronged (2 Timothy 2:24). In fact, we commend ourselves in patience (2 Corinthians 6:6). And guess what? God has given us the power to be patient. We are “strengthened with His power for the attaining of steadfastness and patience” (Colossians 1:11). God puts into us what God wants out of us if we will appropriate it!

Chapter 21

If Money Won't Make You Happy, You Won't Like the Alternative Either

Though crises and battles are not always of our choosing, how we handle them is.

A college professor had the mysterious habit of walking into the lecture hall each morning, removing a tennis ball from his jacket pocket. He would set it on the corner of the podium. After giving the lecture for the day, he would pick up the tennis ball, place it into his jacket pocket, and leave the room.

No one understood why he did this, until one day a student fell asleep during the lecture. The professor never missed a word of his lecture while he walked over to the podium, picked up the tennis ball and threw it, hitting the sleeping student squarely on the top of the head.

The next day, the professor walked into the room, reached into his pocket and removed a baseball. No one ever fell asleep in his class the rest of the semester. [xlix]

Now there's a creative way to getting one's attention!

For many, these financially challenging times have made us feel like we have been hit on the head with a tennis ball. As they say, if you want to get someone's attention, take away his money. Money gives us options and choices. But when our financial tank is running on empty, we get uncomfortable and fearful. That's normal, but let's make sure that we don't let fear run our lives. Though crises and battles are not always of our choosing, how we handle them is.

Perhaps God's purpose in our crisis is not our survival but our education. Author Mike Murdock says, "Financial crisis reveals. Crisis can energize. Crisis can stimulate. Crisis can make us use our faith."[1] Crisis might even cause us to trust in God more than in our money or our job. Usually when these types of crises happen, God has prepared a special way to escape. Why not trust God to reveal it to you?

As I conclude this chapter, I would like to offer this prayer that someone sent to me recently. Here is how the prayer reads: "I pray that three things will be happening to you this week. First of all that in your crisis you will find favor with someone you don't expect. Secondly, I pray that you will be too relevant to be ignored or passed over. Lastly, I pray that if you are in crisis, you will encounter God this week and never be the same."

Why not pray that prayer this week for yourself or someone else? I'm sure it would do us all good. Remember, all people fall down but great people get back up. Oh, I almost forgot. Don't go to sleep in the middle of class!

Chapter 22

How to Turn Distraction into Action

Don't let the distraction of popular logic ruin good theology.

An engineer was crossing a road one day, when a frog called out to him and said, "If you kiss me, I'll turn into a beautiful princess." He bent over, picked up the frog and put it into his pocket.

The frog spoke up again and said, "If you kiss me and I turn back into a beautiful princess, I will stay with you for one week." The engineer took the frog out of his pocket, smiled at it and returned it to his pocket.

The frog then cried out, "If you kiss me and turn me back into a beautiful princess, I'll stay with you for one week and do anything you want." Again, the engineer took the frog out, smiled at it and put it back into his pocket.

Finally, the frog asked, "What is the matter? I've told you I'm a beautiful princess, that I'll stay with you for one week and that I'll do anything you want. Why don't you kiss me?"

The engineer said, "Look, I'm an engineer. I don't have time to have a girlfriend; but a talking frog, now that's cool." [li]

I like that engineer's focus. What might be a trap to most people was not a trap to him. Even in the face of a temptation and distraction, he wouldn't be deterred from his cause. Temptations, enticements and distractions do that. They can put us on detours, and trying to get back on the main road may last a lifetime.

Did you know that right after Jesus' mission to seek and save the lost began, he ran into one of those frogs claiming to be a beautiful princess? He was led into the wilderness and was tempted for 40 days and nights by the original enticer and distracter. In fact, the Bible says during that time He was "tempted in all things as we are, yet without sin" (Hebrews 4:15). Why didn't He fall for the temptations and distractions? His life wasn't just because. His life was be-cause. He had a "be" cause! What was His cause?

First of all, He came from heaven to earth "in order to take away sins" (1John 3:5). You see, God doesn't allow sin in heaven. Why? Well, if we had sin in heaven, then there would be disease, hospitals, mental wards, poverty, robbers, greed, no integrity and the like. Sin causes that kind of stuff.

His second mission was "that He might destroy the works of the evil one" (1John 3:8). Now I know that there is a popular belief that there is no such thing as evil. It's also true that sometimes people blame the devil for all of their shortcomings and missteps. But don't be tempted into believing that the cause of evil does not exist. Evil is the fruit, but Jesus came to get to the root.

Finally, 1 Peter 1:20 declares that Jesus appeared for the sake of you! He appeared that sin might not give the evil one dominion over you. Don't let the distraction of popular logic ruin good theology. He rescued you. He knows your name. He has a place for you in heaven no matter what you have done.

That's what Easter Sunday was all about. A Savior who wouldn't be distracted because He had a cause!

Chapter 23

Learning About Leadership from Storks, Logs and Frogs

Just because you're up in the air and harping on something doesn't mean you're an angel.

This is a most interesting time in world history. Everywhere I go people feel used, violated and even deceived by those in authority in all areas of society. It reminds me of a story by comedian Jackie Mason. "My grandfather always said, 'don't watch your money; watch your health.' So one day while I was watching my health, someone stole my money. It was my grandfather." [lii]

It feels to me like the whole world is simmering. One wonders when it's going to boil.

May I say it this way? Many people in authority have opted for self first, society second. When that happens, personal character and servanthood are sacrificed for winning and controlling. I have heard that Archbishop

Fulton Sheen said, "Civilization is always in danger when those who have never learned how to obey are given the right to command." In other words, if you feel too big for little things, it's probably an indicator that you are too little for big things. Educator and motivational speaker Steve Ventura said, "If there's any concept that's synonymous with leadership it's got to be responsibility." [liii]

Of course, majority populace eventually gets the leaders they vote for, buy from, or listen to. But as Alfred Adler, the Austrian founder of the school of individual psychology, said, "It is easier to fight for one's principles than to live up to them." [liv] This observation might easily be applied to today's long-on-promises-but-short-on-delivery popular leaders. Just because you're up in the air and harping on something doesn't mean you're an angel. The frustration is overwhelming and the consequences often severe.

Aesop tells the story of the frogs who wanted a king. They annoyed Jupiter with their request until he finally tossed a log into the pond. For a while the frogs were happy with their new leader.

Soon, however, they discovered that they could jump up and down on their leader and run all over him. He offered no resistance and gave no response. He merely floated back and forth on the pond, a practice that finally exasperated the frogs who were really sincere about wanting "strong leadership."

So back to Jupiter they went, complaining about their log leader and appealing for much stronger administrative oversight. Jupiter was weary of the tiresome frogs, so this time he gave them a stork that stood tall above the members of the group. He certainly had the appearance of a leader. The frogs were quite happy with the new situation. Their leader stalked around the pond making impressive noises and attracting great attention. Their joy turned to sorrow, however, and then to panic when very soon the stork began eating his subjects. [lv]

Frogs, let's quit swinging back and forth between logs and storks. Frogs, the Bible tells us what a real leader is like. "Kings like to throw their weight around, and people in authority like to give themselves fancy titles. It's not going to be that way for you (disciples). Let the senior among you become like the junior; let the leader act the part of a servant" (Philippians 2:3-4 Message).

Leaders don't gather for themselves; they give to others without agendas, earmarks and e-mail attachments. That takes character and servanthood. Learn from others' mistakes — the second mouse gets the cheese!

Chapter 24

Meet What You Will Never Get Rid Of

Conscience does not make or pass the law.
Conscience bears witness to the law.
—Warren Wiersbe

A burglar who needed money to pay his income taxes decided to rob the safe in a store. On the safe door he was very pleased to find a note reading, "Please don't use dynamite. The safe is not locked. Just turn the knob." He did so. Instantly, a heavy sandbag fell on him, the entire premises was lit by floodlights, and alarms started clanging. As the police carried him out on a stretcher, he was heard moaning, "My confidence in human nature has been rudely shaken." [lvi]

We may stifle it; we might quench it, hurt it or even defile it. However, we will never be able to escape it. It will always be there, attaching itself to the highest standard we know. Everyone has heard it speak to us, congratulate us, convict us, remind us or try to guide us. What am I talking about? Let's meet our conscience. Charles Wesley called conscience, "a principle within of watchful godly fear."[lvii]

In the Greek language, conscience means "to know with." The word conscience was used by the Greek people in their everyday conversation. It meant "the pain that you feel when you do wrong." Conscience is that inner faculty that indicates to us whether our actions are right or wrong, according to the standards we have in our heart.

Bible teacher Warren Wiersbe notes, "Conscience is not the law; conscience bears witness to the law. Conscience is not the standard; conscience bears witness to the standard. Conscience is judicial. Conscience does not make or pass the law. Conscience bears witness to the law."[lviii] You see, conscience can be our guide to God's highest and our best if we have the right standards." Pretty heady stuff, huh?

When we cheat on an examination, tell a lie, or do something that we simply should not do, our conscience bothers us. Something inside of us says, "Dude, you missed it!" Of course, like the burglar above, we may have abused our conscience so much that it doesn't bother us anymore in the really important areas of life that bring peace and prosperity. That is what the Bible calls an evil, defiled or weak conscience. Our conscience can only respond to the standards it has. That's why it's important to have the best standard.

Some believe that conscience comes from behind us, that is, from our evolution. Some believe that conscience comes from around us, that is, from society-based standards. Some believe conscience comes from within us, that is, from our upbringing or family standards. Remember, society or our upbringing may give us standards, but it doesn't give us a conscience.

The Bible says in Romans 2:14-15 that conscience comes from above us. Conscience is found in people everywhere in the world. It has a common source, and that common source is God. God gave all mankind a facility called the conscience together with the best standard for operating the conscience.

Indeed, our conscience is our guide. It can help us or hurt us depending on the standard we choose for it.

Hint: Don't force your conscience to malfunction … read and live by the Bible.

Chapter 25

Lies Have to be Covered Up — Truth Can Run Around Naked

When a culture of half-truths develops, we tend to build cases on half-truths, adding more half-truths to the original half-truths until we are far from the real truth.

The title of this article is a quote by the late country singer Johnny Cash. Let me illustrate what he is saying with a story about aging.

I went to the doctor for my yearly physical. The nurse started with certain basics. "How much do you weigh?" she asked.

"135," I replied. The nurse put me on the scale. It turns out my weight is 160.

The nurse asked, "Your height?"

I replied, "5 feet, 6 inches." The nurse checked and saw that I only measure 5 feet, 3 inches. Then she took my blood pressure and told me that it was very high.

“Of course it’s high!” I screamed. “When I came in here I was tall and slender! Now I’m short and fat!”

She put me on Prozac. [lix]

As they say, denial is not a river in Egypt.

There are all kinds of dangers in refusing to accept real truth. One danger is that the longer we tell a lie, the more we believe it. Soon we can’t separate truth from falsehood. I know some fishermen who do that.

Another danger is that one can suppress the truth with a lie by redefining truth. We have become a culture of “spin.” The end-justifies-the-means approach to life causes the whole of society to underachieve. Solving problems requires the rock of truth, not the sand of half-truths and destructive emotions.

Another downside of falsehood is that good relationships between people and institutions diminish. Why? Lying destroys trust, and trust is the currency of all relationships. People become pawns in other people’s plans, causes and agendas. There’s nothing on which to build a relationship.
Finally, when a culture of half-truths develops, we tend to build cases on half-truths, adding more half-truths to the original half-truths until we are far from the real truth. Like a ship without a compass, it leads us to where no one wants to go.

So lies cause us to cover up, hide things and justify ourselves. When Adam and Eve first missed God’s mark and discovered they were naked, the first thing they did was cover up. They found some big fig leaves and hid themselves from God and each other. Then Adam lied and added some spin and interest on his “reality.”

"The woman, whom You gave me, made me eat the fruit." Notice his lie, justified by blaming God. Then he hid behind the fig leaf of being a victim when he was responsible. The result was that Eve became the real victim. However, Eve did the same blame shifting. She pointed at the snake. As I said in an earlier chapter, Adam blamed Eve, Eve blamed the snake and the snake didn't have a leg to stand on. Blame shifting is mostly shame shifting. Adam and Eve came into the garden together but left alone because they would not allow the truth to set them free.

What is the solution? All Adam and Eve had to do was take responsibility, not shift responsibility. The Bible says in 1 John 1:9 that if we confess our sins to God, He is faithful and just to forgive our sins and cleanse us of all unrighteousness. And in John 8:32 Jesus tells us the truth will set us free. It takes courage to unlock ourselves from the prison of falsehood. But, we can do it. I know we can!

Chapter 26

Life and Leadership Lessons Learned From C-130 Cargo Planes and F16 Fighters

Even with all the razzle-dazzle, glamour and glitz that go along with the Top Gun crowd, the F-16 has to refuel from the C-130. That drives F-16 guys like me crazy!

A C-130 Hercules cargo plane was lumbering along when a cocky F-16 flashed by. The jet jockey decided to show off. The fighter jock told the C-130 pilot, "Watch this!" and promptly went into a barrel roll followed by a steep climb. He then finished with a sonic boom as he broke the sound barrier.

"What did you think of that?" asked the F-16 pilot.

The C-130 pilot said, "That was impressive, but watch this!" The C-130 droned along for about five minutes and then the C-130 pilot came back on the radio and said, "What did you think of that?"

Puzzled, the F-16 pilot asked, "What the heck did you do?" The C-130 pilot chuckled. "I stood up and stretched my legs, walked to the back of the plane, went to the bathroom, and then got a cup of coffee and a cinnamon bun." [lx]

That's quite a story, isn't it? Those C-130 tortoise-type people just keep on going forward while the F-16 hare-type people are going upwards, downwards, forwards and backwards. Sometimes, they almost kill themselves showing off what they can do.

Now don't get me wrong. I think those F-16s are very effective and make great escorts for the C-130s. However, even with all the razzle-dazzle, glamour and glitz that go along with the Top Gun crowd, the F-16 has to refuel from the C-130. That drives F-16 guys like me crazy! While we are trying to impress the C-130 crowd, they have switched on the autopilot, are sitting in the back of the plane eating donuts, enjoying the ride and not getting airsick. Go figure!

This story reminds me of Mary and Martha in Luke 10:38-42. Jesus was at their home speaking to folks in their village. Martha was in the kitchen doing flips, steep climbs, creating sonic booms and consuming heaps of fuel trying to get supper ready. Mary, in the meantime, was sitting at Jesus' feet, listening, learning, getting "refueled" and enjoying the ride.

Martha interrupted Jesus and said, "Master, don't you care that my sister has abandoned the kitchen to me? Tell her to lend me a hand." The Master said, "Martha, dear Martha, you're fussing far too much and getting yourself worked up over nothing. One thing only is essential and Mary has chosen it — it's the main course, and it won't be taken from her." [lxi]

Here's a God lesson as well as a leadership lesson. He is the Vine and we humans are the branches. The branch needs to be attached to the vine to produce fruit. It may seem to us F-16 humans as if God is moving slower than a C-130. Remember, don't detach. God will get you there, and you might even enjoy the ride.

Oh, by the way, I married one of those C-130 types. It's just not fair!

Chapter 27

What We Reflect Is What We Are ... A Thousand Times

That which is on the inside of us "often" shows up in our outward appearance. Mirrors "don't" make news — they report news.

A Japanese folktale called "The House of 1,000 Mirrors" goes like this:

Long ago in a small, faraway village, there was place known as the House of 1,000 Mirrors. A small, happy little dog learned of this place and decided to visit. When he arrived, he bounced happily up the stairs to the doorway of the house. He looked through the doorway with his ears lifted high and his tail wagging as fast as it could. To his great surprise, he found himself staring at 1,000 other happy little dogs with their tails wagging just as fast as his.

He smiled a great smile, and was answered with 1,000 great smiles just as warm and friendly. As he left the house, he thought to himself, "This is a wonderful place. I will come back and visit it often."

In this same village, another little dog, who was not quite as happy as the first one, decided to visit the house. He slowly climbed the stairs and hung his head low as he looked into the door. When he saw the 1,000 unfriendly looking dogs staring back at him, he growled at them and was horrified to see 1,000 little dogs growling back at him. As he left, he thought to himself, "That is a horrible place, and I will never go back there again." [lxii]

Lesson: All the faces in the world are mirrors. What kinds of reflections do you see in the faces of the people you meet?

It's interesting how a mirror reflects what we look like and perhaps even who we are. After all, that which is on the inside of us often shows up in our outward appearance. Mirrors don't make news — they report news.

Proverbs 23:7 says that as a man thinks in his heart, so he becomes. A mirror reflects and reports what is going on in the inside of us that has leaked to the outside of us. If our constant inward attitude is like the song "Raindrops Keep Falling on My Head" or "Make the World Go Away," there will be multitudes of others seeing us that way. If our constant inward attitude is like the song "Oh! What a Beautiful Morning!" then others will see us that way too.

Which is the better option? You can decide but I would rather be positive. Frankly, I don't like the other option. Why? We become a servant to the choices we make. Once we choose to be negative on the inside, we become servants to that choice. Like both dogs in the House of Mirrors story, what we project will multiply in our own mind. Other people also will see us that way.

Think of it. We will attract others just like us, too. If the people around us tend to be negative and make us unhappy, it's not their fault. It's our fault.

We drew them to us. We allow them to remain.

That's why successful people are naturally drawn to other successful people, kind people tend to hang with kind people, and hardworking people hang with other hardworking people. Get the message?

What we reflect is what we project and maybe even who we are … a thousand times.

Chapter 28

Nothing Is So Simple that It Can't Be Misunderstood

It takes going to extra lengths to make sure that what we say moves from speech to understanding. In other words, output is not outcome.

Isn't the quote by Freeman Teague Jr. that forms the title of this article a great concept? In these days of spin and polarization, clear accurate communication is essential. One little mistake can cause a plethora of misunderstandings, offenses and hurt. Former CEO of Intel Corporation Andrew Grove notes that how well we communicate is determined not by how we say things, but by how well we are understood. [lxiii] Understanding is in the mind of the receiver. The transmitter had better be aware that communication is two-way, not one-way. Let me illustrate what an unintended miscommunication can do.

A Minneapolis, Minnesota, couple decided to go to Florida to thaw out during a particularly icy winter. They planned to stay at the same hotel where they spent their honeymoon twenty years earlier. Because of hectic schedules, it was difficult to coordinate their travel schedules. So, the husband left Minnesota and flew south to sunny Florida on Thursday, with his wife flying the following day. The husband checked into the hotel. There was a computer in his room so he decided to send an e-mail to his wife. However, he accidentally left out one letter in her e-mail address, and without realizing his error, sent the e-mail.

Meanwhile, somewhere in Houston, Texas, a widow had just returned home from her husband's funeral. He was a minister who was called home to glory following a heart attack. The widow decided to check her e-mail expecting messages from relatives and friends. After reading the first message, she screamed and fainted.

The widow's son rushed into the room, found his mother on the floor, and saw the computer screen which read:

To: My Loving Wife
Subject: I've arrived
Date: October 16, 2005

The text read, "I know you're surprised to hear from me. They have computers down here now and you are allowed to send e-mails to your loved ones. I've just arrived and have been checked in. I've seen that everything has been prepared for your arrival tomorrow. Looking forward to seeing you then! Hope your journey is as uneventful as mine was.

"P.S. Sure is hot down here!" [lxiv]

I realize that we can't always know where others are coming from when they're talking to us. Just look at "Mars" men and "Venus" women. Truth, both live on Earth. It takes going to extra lengths to make sure that what we say moves from speech to understanding. In other words, output is not outcome. Output is talk or speech. Outcome is the communication and understanding of what was spoken. Wealthy industrialist Andrew Carnegie said, "As I grow older, I pay less attention to what men say. I just watch what they do." [lxv] One-way rhetoric does not equal two-way communication, whether man-to-man or woman-to-woman or between the genders.

The great thing about God is that He is clear in His communication. God doesn't try to say something without saying it. He is loving when He needs to be loving, confrontational when He needs to be confrontational, direct when He needs to be direct, but above all, He is always truthful. We may not like what He says, but it is always for our best. He is the ultimate reconciliation expert. His first approach to avoid a misunderstanding is always "Come now, let us reason together." [lxvi]

Chapter 29

Postponing Today What Could Be Done Today

The problem with doing nothing is that nothing gets done!

Here's a thought you will enjoy.

Mortal: What is a million years like to you?
God: Like one second.
Mortal: What is a million dollars like to you?
God: Like one penny.
Mortal: Can I have a penny?
God: Just a second.

Well, God does have time on His side but down here on earth, time isn't always on our side. Sometimes we make decisions too quickly. That's called impulsiveness. Conversely, sometimes we can be much too slow in making decisions. That's called procrastination. We postpone today what could or should be done today. Procrastination can be caused by laziness, fear, the paralysis of analysis, circumstances and the like. But here, I'm talking about the procrastination caused by laziness or what the Bible calls slothfulness.

I recently saw someone wearing a T-shirt that stated, "We are forming the Procrastination Society tomorrow." That reminded me of the Procrastinator's Creed which I will list below for you. Warning: You may wish to delay reading this until you have more free time.

1. I believe that if anything is worth doing, it would have been done already.
2. I shall never move quickly, except to avoid more work or find excuses.
3. I will never rush into a job without a lifetime of consideration.
4. I shall meet all of my deadlines directly in proportion to the amount of bodily injury I could expect to receive from missing them.
5. I firmly believe that tomorrow holds the possibility for new technologies, astounding discoveries, and a reprieve from my obligations.
6. I believe that all deadlines are unreasonable regardless of the amount of time given.
7. If at first you don't succeed, there is always next year.
8. I shall always decide not to decide, unless of course I decide to change my mind.
9. I shall always begin, start, initiate, take the first step, and/or write the first word, when I get around to it.
10. I will never put off till tomorrow, what I can forget about forever. [lxviii]

Obviously this creed overstates procrastination to an extreme, but don't miss the message. In crisis times like these, avoiding responsibility is not the answer. Sticking your head into the sand is not the answer. Procrastination or impulsiveness is not the answer. That only brings more defeat and frustration. Proverbs 13:4 says, "Indolence (laziness) wants it all and gets nothing; the energetic have something to show for their lives." The problem with doing nothing is that nothing gets done!

Oh, by the way, God is an expert at getting people through times like these. He loves everybody, but He strengthens the energetic and He rewards the diligent, even when wrong decisions were made. I like to say it this way: If it's going to be, it starts with me …. and He!

Finally, keep going, even if God says, "Just a second."

Chapter 30

Pursuing Excellence in Average Times

Little things do matter in the long run.

A zookeeper wanted to get some extra animals for his zoo, so he decided to compose a letter. The only problem was that he didn't know the plural of "mongoose." He started the letter: "To whom it may concern, I need two mongeese." No, that wouldn't work, so he tried again: "To whom it may concern, I need two mongooses." That didn't look right to him. Finally, he got an idea on how to start the letter: "To whom it may concern, I need a mongoose, and while you are at it, send me another one." [lxix]

I like that. The gentleman wanted to use the correct grammar and spelling. You could say that he cared enough to be as excellent as possible in his composition.

One Bible verse that I have never forgotten is in the sixth chapter of Romans. The last part of the verse says, "Be excellent at what is good and innocent of evil" (Romans 16:19). Just think of how much better a place the world would be if we all would be excellent in what is good and innocent in evil. Excellence is a wonderful ally to have by your side in these average-yet-challenging times. Excellence helps you to stand out by becoming outstanding. Excellence attracts promotion, prosperity, leadership and influence. Right now excellence can really work for us if we will let it.

People are looking for examples of excellence. The Bible talks of Daniel who had an "extraordinary spirit." Daniel had such integrity, wisdom, and favor that even the government was in awe of his testimonial life. You see, little things do matter in the long run. It's the little things that separate one sports team from another. Excellence in the little things gives that slight advantage that is often the difference between winning and losing. Excellence in one company as compared to another often is the difference between a profit and a loss.

Jesus had an excellent spirit too. There was nothing that any enemy could accuse Him of. Jesus declared in the fourteenth chapter of John, "The ruler of this world is coming, but he has nothing in Me" (John 14:30). Jesus was excellent in what is good and innocent in evil. Now, admittedly we are not Jesus Christ, but we can certainly all do better in striving toward excellence and innocence, especially if we have the life of Christ indwelling and empowering us.

Excellence often starts with an attitude. Here is a poem by John Mason that points the way to an attitude of excellence. It's called "Do More …":

Do more than exist, live.
Do more than hear, listen.
Do more than agree, cooperate.
Do more than talk, communicate.
Do more than grow, bloom.
Do more than spend, invest.
Do more than think, create.
Do more than work, excel.
Do more than share, give.
Do more than decide, discern.
Do more than consider, commit.
Do more than forgive, forget.
Do more than help, serve.
Do more than coexist, reconcile.
Do more than sing, worship.
Do more than think, plan.
Do more than dream, do.
Do more than see, perceive.
Do more than read, apply.
Do more than receive, reciprocate.
Do more than choose, focus.
Do more than wish, believe.
Do more than advise, help.
Do more than speak, impart.
Do more than encourage, inspire.
Do more than add, multiply.
Do more than change, improve.
Do more than reach, stretch.
Do more than ponder, pray. [lxx]

Aspire to inspire before you expire!

Chapter 31

Saying the Right Thing at the Right Time

The real art of conversation is not only to say the right thing at the right place but to leave unsaid the wrong thing at the tempting moment.
— Lady Dorothy Fanny Nevill

I think you will like this story. It illustrates an important concept that will work for us. Read on!

Jack wakes up with a huge hangover after attending his company's Grand Opening Party. Jack is not normally a drinker, but the drinks didn't taste like alcohol at all. He doesn't even remember how he got home from the party and who dropped him off. As bad as he is feeling, he wonders if he did something wrong.

Jack has to force himself to open his eyes. The first thing he sees is a couple of aspirin next to a glass of water on the side table. Next to the aspirin is a red rose. Jack sits up and sees his clothing in front of him, all cleaned and pressed. He looks around the room and sees that it is in perfect order, spotlessly clean. So is the rest of the house.

He takes the aspirin and cringes when he sees a huge black eye staring back at him in the bathroom mirror. Then he notices a note hanging on the corner of the mirror written in red with little hearts on it and a lipstick kiss mark from his wife. The note reads, "Honey, breakfast is on the stove, and I left early to get groceries to make you your favorite dinner tonight. I love you darling! Love, Jillian."

He stumbles to the kitchen and sure enough, there is a hot breakfast with steaming hot coffee and the morning newspaper. His son appears at the table. Jack asks, "Son, what happened last night?"

"Well, you came home after 3:00 A.M., drunk out of your mind. You fell over the coffee table and broke it, then you got sick in the hallway and you got that black eye when you ran into the door."

Confused, Jack asks his son, "So, why is everything in such perfect order and so clean? I have a rose, and breakfast is on the table waiting for me." His son replies, "Oh that! Mom dragged you to the bedroom and when she tried to take your pants off, you screamed, 'Leave me alone, lady, I'm married!' "

Summing this up: Broken coffee table … $239.00; hot breakfast … $4.20; two aspirin … $.38; saying the right thing, at the right time … priceless! [lxxi]

I hope you weren't offended by this story, because it makes a great point. Saying the right thing at the right time is priceless! Saying the right thing at the right time is also wise. Lady Dorothy Fanny Nevill once noted, "The real art of conversation is not only to say the right thing at the right place but to leave unsaid the wrong thing at the tempting moment."[lxxii]

American advice columnist Ann Landers observed, “The trouble with talking too fast is you may say something you haven’t thought of yet.” Ouch! Been there, done that, got the T-shirt!

The Bible, as usual, contains the best wisdom you can get on this subject: “Like apples of gold in settings of silver is a word spoken in right circumstances” (Proverbs 25:11). If something goes without saying, let it.

Chapter 32

Stress Management For Dummies ... and Smarties!

So many folks today are like a billiard table with balls all over the board. From time to time, take the time to re-rack the billiard balls.

A lecturer, when explaining stress management to an audience, raised a glass of water and asked, "How heavy is this glass of water?" Answers called out ranged from 20 grams to 500 grams. The lecturer replied, "The absolute weight doesn't matter. It depends on how long you hold it. If I hold it for a minute, that's not a problem. If I hold it for an hour, I'll have an ache in my right arm. If I hold it for a day, you will have to call an ambulance. In each case, it's the same weight. However, the longer I hold it, the heavier it becomes."

He continued, "And that is the way it is with stress management. If we carry our burdens all the time, sooner or later, as the burden becomes increasingly heavy, we won't be able to carry on. When we are refreshed, we can carry on with the burden. So before you return home tonight, put down the burden of work. Don't carry it home. You can pick it up tomorrow!"[lxxiii]

Now, there's some good advice. If you never stop, you can't start! Sometimes, you have to come apart, or you will ... come apart!

Here's some logic for the overly stressed. Since it's the early worm that gets eaten by the early bird ... sleep late! So many folks today are like a billiard table with balls all over the board. From time to time, take the time to re-rack the billiard balls. Some people live their lives as though some mistakes are too much fun to make only once. Sometimes it seems like my sole purpose in life is simply to serve as a warning to others. Got the message?

Jesus taught stress management. Remember the Bible story about when the disciples were in the middle of a sea, in the middle of the night and in the middle of the perfect storm? [lxxiv] I'll bet their blood pressure was 190 over 130. Then Jesus appears, walking on water. They thought it was a ghost.

Let's review. It's the middle of the night, in the middle of the perfect storm, in the middle of the sea and now they have a ghost walking around on water. Mercury rising! Now it's 210 over 150!

Yet, even in the middle of the storm, Jesus was there. His words were, "Take courage, it is I; do not be afraid." In today's lingo it would read, "Surf's up ... cool it dudes ... situation under control!" Sure enough, the storm calmed right down. The lesson here is, don't let the storm on the outside of you get inside of you! Great advice for the storm-challenged, huh?

Jesus' advice was to relax when life gets too stressed. He says in Matthew 6, "Instead of looking at the fashions, walk out into the fields and look at the wildflowers. They never primp or shop, but have you ever seen color and design quite like it? The ten best-dressed men and women in the country look shabby alongside them. If God gives such attention to the appearance of wildflowers — most of which are never even seen —don't you think that He will attend to you, take pride in what you do and do His best for you? What I'm trying to say here is relax, to not be so occupied with getting, so you can respond to God's giving." [lxxv]

My advice: When life gets too stressed, put down the glass, sleep late and remember there is one less early worm.

Chapter 33

Take What You Know With You

Peter went from fishing for fish to fishing for men. David went from shepherding sheep to shepherding a nation.

A gynecologist had become so fed up with malpractice insurance, threats from lawyers and HMO paperwork that he became burned out. Hoping to try another career where skillful hands would be beneficial, he decided to become a mechanic. He went to a technical college, signed up for classes, attended diligently and learned all he could.

When the time for the practical exam came, he prepared carefully for weeks and completed the exam with tremendous skill. When the results came back, he was surprised to find that he had obtained a score of 150 percent. Fearing an error, he called the instructor saying, "I don't want to appear ungrateful for such an outstanding result, but I wonder if there is an error in the grade."

The instructor said, "During the exam, you took the engine apart perfectly which was worth 50 percent of the total mark. You put the engine back together again perfectly, which is also worth 50 percent of the mark. This equaled an A."

After a pause, the instructor added, "I gave you an extra 50 percent because you did it all through the muffler, which I've never seen in my entire career." [lxxvi]

Now, I know what you are thinking. How am I going to apply the gynecologist story to a biblical principle?

Many of us are under stress due to work layoffs or career or field-of-specialty changes. We tend to think the worst when considering what we will do next. But remember that you have a skill set. The gynecologist was skillful with his hands, and as the story above points out, that skill was not limited to just medical practice. It could be used in multitudes of careers and jobs. In other words, don't limit yourself to one industry or business. Somebody out there needs what you contain.

If you are good at sales, take that skill and go to work in another industry where selling is required. If you are effective in management, take it elsewhere. Many times you end up better off than you were before. Seasons of crisis can bring us into seasons of creativity that can change our lives forever. Besides, the Holy Spirit is attracted to creativity. God can make it happen.

In the Bible, Peter went from fishing for fish to fishing for men. David went from shepherding sheep to shepherding a nation. Abraham went from a father of a small family in Babylon to the father of a large nation called Israel. Nehemiah graduated from serving a man to serving cities.

Paul went from reciting the Word of God to learning directly from the God of the Word. In modern times, the Wright Brothers transitioned from making bicycles to making history.

Same skill set, different arena. Taking what they had and applying it in another context was the best thing they ever did. Sometimes we look at life through the big end of the telescope, and the stars look distant and dim. God says to turn the telescope around! With our skill set and God's direction, anything is possible.

Chapter 34

Today's Market Activity from a Unique Perspective

Worry is as wicked as swearing. Swearing is taking God's name in vain. Worry is taking God's promises in vain.
—John Maxwell

Wow! For the last few weeks the world has been riding an emotional roller coaster financially. You can't blame anyone for being on edge during these times. Everyone likes stability and security, that's normal. Many folks feel like "Stock market, don't bother me; I'm trying to live happily ever after."

Maybe this small chapter can bring some inspiration to you today. So let's start with another look at today's market activity. You probably won't see this in your local newspaper.

"Helium was up. Feathers were down. Paper was stationary. Fluorescent tubing was dimmed in light trading. Knives were up sharply. Cows steered into a bull market. Pencils lost a few points. Hiking equipment was trailing. Elevators rose, while escalators continued their slow decline. Weights were up in heavy trading. Light switches were off.

"Mining equipment hit rock bottom. Diapers and nappies remained unchanged. Shipping lines stayed at even keel. The market for raisins dried up. Soft drinks fizzled. Caterpillar stock inched up a bit. Balloon prices were inflated. Toilet paper touched a new bottom." [lxxvii]

Maybe you are thinking my jokes touched a new bottom.

As I write this chapter, I'm looking at a sign in my office. It says the following: "Good morning. This is God! I will be handling all your problems today. I will not need your help. So, have a good day."

Do you know what? That sign has been there for years. It was there during September 11, 2001. It was there during the housing and real estate boom and bust. It was there when a business partner went bankrupt because of the economy jeopardizing everything that we had worked toward for 40 years. It was there when our second granddaughter was in the Neonatal Intensive Care Unit at Phoenix Children's Hospital for 25 days. Get the message?

Someone said that worry is what gives small things big shadows. Our hopes pull us one way and our worries pull us the other way and we are pulled apart. The root word for worry in the Bible is the word "strangle." When worries come, don't go with them if you don't want to be strangled emotionally. John Maxwell once said that worry is "as wicked as swearing. Swearing is taking God's name in vain. Worry is taking God's promises in vain."

What I have learned (not too quickly or easily at times) is that God is good, God is faithful, and you can trust God, especially in times like these. The Bible declares that God's plans for us are for our welfare; plans that give us a future and a hope. [lxxviii] Maybe everything will turn out fine or maybe it won't. But later we will see what God was doing in the midst of the storm and see that it was for our benefit and God's purposes.

Maybe being temporarily upside down in our finances can turn us right side up with heaven permanently.

So, have a good day!

Chapter 35

The Discovery of Purpose Is the Discovery of Life

God had a divine design when He had you and me in mind.

Let's start with a story.

A sidewalk preacher stood on a soapbox downtown and started a rousing sermon on salvation. "Brothers and sisters, if you want to go to heaven, come stand by me!"

Half of those standing around joined the preacher. He went on, raising his voice and fervor again. "Brothers and sisters, if you want to go to heaven, come over and stand with me!"

Half of those left came over, and the preacher continued, ending up with another call of heaven. This time all but one man came over.

"Brother!" cried the preacher, "Don't you want to go to heaven when you die?"

The man responded, "Oh sure, when I die. I thought you were taking a load up now!" [lxxix]

Acts 13:36 says, "For David, after he had served the purpose of God in his own generation, feel asleep, and was laid among his fathers." This short verse holds a powerful truth. You see, David did not go to be with the Lord until after he had discovered and fulfilled the purpose of his life for his own generation. That is called "dying."

That is what God has in mind for us. We are here on this earth, on purpose and for a purpose by the God of purpose. We have a God-given destiny and assignment. Author and motivational speaker Dr. Myles Munroe says that our existence is evidence that this generation needs something that our life contains. God had a "divine design" when He had you and me in mind. He had an intent, a reason for being, for each one of us. We are the way we are because of why we are.

You see, like King David and Queen Esther, we all were born "for such a time as this" with a purpose. [lxxx] In other words, when the Lord made you, he looked at you and said, "I'll never do that again!" You're special, you're unique and you're one of a kind … for a purpose.

Chuck Pierce defines destiny this way: "Destiny is a pre-determined course of events that has been decreed, assigned and dedicated in advance for a particular purpose or place, so prosperity ultimately occurs." [lxxxi] Prosperity is fulfilling the purposes of God for our generation. Destiny is the ultimate place where God wants to take us and the steps that take us there. That's not only powerful, it's true.

Proverbs 16:4 says, "The Lord has made everything for its own purpose." Destiny is not some cosmic force or random circumstances; destiny is determined by the God who made us. His Word uses the term "predestined" many times so we won't miss it.

So, we have a purpose. When we discover and fulfill it, good things happen. Zig Ziglar said that knowing our purpose moves us from a "wandering generality to a meaningful specific." [lxxxii] It's been said that loneliness is not the absence of affection; loneliness is the absence of direction.

If you don't know your purpose and assignment, ask God and pray. After all, if you want to know the purpose of a thing, never ask the thing.

Chapter 36

The Man Who Pursued and Got It All

All his trivial pursuits were "vanity and striving after wind."

In today's world most people are looking for the perfect partner, the perfect job, the perfect life, the perfect government, the perfect environment … the perfect everything. There's nothing wrong with wanting to make things better, but seeking perfection in everything is a trivial pursuit. The story below illustrates my point:

A friend asked a man why he never married. The man replied, "Well, I guess I just never met the right woman. I guess I've was looking for the perfect girl."

"Oh, come on now," said the friend, "Surely you have met at least one girl that you wanted to marry."

“Yes, there was a very special girl once. She was the one and only perfect girl that I ever met. She was just the right everything. She was the perfect girl for me.”

“Well, why didn’t you marry her,” asked the friend.

He replied, “She was looking for the perfect man.”

The Bible tells the story of a man named Solomon. He was the wealthiest man on earth and could buy anything and do anything he wanted. He set out to find contentment and meaning in life.

His pursuits are recorded in the Bible in Ecclesiastes chapter 2. In verse 3, Solomon says, “I explored with my heart how to stimulate my body with wine … and how to take hold of folly.”

Our world is full of heaps of people who do that. Excessive alcohol, drugs and stimulants will never heal life’s wounds or give meaningful answers to life’s questions.

In verse 4, Solomon says, “I enlarged my works. I built houses for myself, and planted in them all kinds of trees.” He tried better homes and gardens to see if life was about owning the most expensive house on the block.

He sought to find fulfillment in nature and the environment. “I made gardens and parks for myself … I made ponds of water for myself from which to irrigate a forest of growing trees.” He was going green thinking that it would fill that void in him. Green is fine but green will only temporarily meet one’s need at best. It’s not sustainable that way.

Solomon’s next trivial pursuit was trying to possess the biggest and wealthiest business in the world. In verses 7 and 8 he says, "Also I possessed flocks and herds larger than all who preceded me … I collected silver and gold and the treasures of kings and provinces." That was like backing up and running over the iceberg again.

Then in verse 8 he reports that he tried every kind of sex and excess pleasure. "I provided male and female singers and the pleasures of men — many concubines." Nope, that was toxic and empty, too.

Finally, Solomon became the most famous and wealthy man who ever lived from the beginning of history. That didn't satisfy him either. Solomon says that all his trivial pursuits were "vanity and striving after wind." Happiness, contentment and the meaning of life were like a greased pig to Solomon. Every time he thought he caught the pig, it squirted right out of his hands. Sound familiar?

Where did Solomon end up? His bottom line and the only thing that will ever fill the God-shaped void in him and us is this: "Fear God and keep His commandments, because this applies to every person" (Ecclesiastes 12:13).

That greased pig just got caught!

Chapter 37

Truthfulness: Earning Future Trust by Accurately Reporting Past Facts

We may have a vested interest in telling just the part of a story that we want people to hear.

Have you noticed that things sometimes get lost in the translation? One person hears one thing and another person hears another depending on how well we are listening. Or we may have a vested interest in telling just the part of a story that we want people to hear. Or maybe there's just plain confusion on both the sending and the receiving end.

Let me give you some examples of mixed messages from moviemaker Samuel Goldwyn, who was notorious for his misuses of the English language. Hang on, here we go:

"An oral contract isn't worth the paper it's written on."
"Gentlemen, include me out."
"Anyone who goes to a psychiatrist needs to have his head examined."
"I read part of it all the way through."
"I had a great idea this morning but I didn't like it."
"Give me a couple years, and I'll make that actress an overnight success."
"A hospital is no place to be sick." [lxxxiii]

I think you get the message. He wasn't deceptive. He was, shall we say, divergent.

Now let me give you a great example on half-truths intended to be deceptive. This is the story of Pepe Rodriguez. It's by Tony Campolo, quoted in a book called *Hot Illustrations* for Youth Talks by Wayne Rice (Zondervan).

Pepe Rodriguez, one of the most notorious bank robbers in the early settling of the American West, lived just across the border in Mexico. He regularly crept into Texas towns to rob banks, returning to Mexico just before the Texas Rangers could catch him.

The frustrated lawmen were so embarrassed by this that they illegally crossed the border into Mexico. Eventually, they cornered Pepe in a Mexican bar that he frequented. Unfortunately, Pepe couldn't speak any English, so the lawmen asked the bartender to translate for them.

The bartender explained to Pepe who these men were, and Pepe began to shake with fear. The Texas Rangers, with their guns drawn, told the bartender to ask Pepe where he had hidden all the money he had stolen from the Texas banks. "Tell him if he doesn't tell us where the money is right now, we're going to shoot him dead on the spot!"

The bartender translated all this for Pepe. Immediately, Pepe explained in Spanish that the money was hidden in the town well. They could find the money by counting down seventeen stones from the handle, and behind the seventeenth stone was all the loot he had stolen.

The bartender then turned to the Rangers and said in English, "Pepe is a very brave man. He says that you are a bunch of stinking pigs, and that he is not afraid to die."

Do you see what I mean when I say that sometimes things get lost in translation?

My good friends at Character First, a character-based leadership development program, make a distinction between truthfulness and deception. "Truthfulness is earning future trust by accurately reporting past facts." [lxxxiv] Did you notice the word facts? Many times in today's world, an individual's version of truth may trump the actual facts of a situation, and that is a shame. As Johnny Cash sang in his song "Farmer's Almanac," "Lies have to be covered up, truth can run around naked."

How do we make our lives, relationships and community better? Let's make sure that we are not only getting the truth, but also communicating the truth to others … factually.

Chapter 38

Embracing and Investing In Generation Next

Many over-35s are still trying to make a credit-card call on a rotary telephone.

Here's a story about investing in the next generation I think you will enjoy, especially the women:

I was out walking with my 4-year-old granddaughter. She picked up something off of the ground and started to put it in her mouth. I took the item away from her and I asked her not to do that. "Why?" my granddaughter asked.

"Because it has been on the ground. You don't know where it has been, it's dirty, and it probably has germs," I replied.

At this point, my granddaughter looked at me with total admiration and asked, "Grandma, how do you know all this stuff? You are so smart."

I was thinking quickly. "All Grandmas know this stuff. It's on the Grandma Test. You have to know it or they don't let you be a Grandma."

We walked along in silence for two or three minutes, but she was evidently pondering this new information. "Oh, I get it!" My granddaughter beamed. "So if you don't pass the test, you have to be the Grandpa."

"Exactly," I replied. [lxxxv]

And all the Grandmas say, "Amen!"

Recently I attended a church stuff conference in Honolulu, Hawaii. Pastor Mel Mullen of Red Deer, Alberta, Canada, shared a story about his church that impacted me. Pastor Mel has a successful group of churches throughout Canada called Word of Life. The main church in Red Deer is healthy, with all of the attendance figures, financial budget and influence that you would expect to see in a successful church.

The problem was that Pastor Mel is in his late 50s and half of his church had grown older with him. He had a staff of 35 years-old-and-under leaders that were trying to help him grow a church for over-35-years-old congregants. They had a church whose entire aim was to feed older Christian "spiritual giraffes." The question he asked himself was, "Can 35 years-old-and-under leaders grow an over-35-years-old church?"

His conclusion was that his church was going to be a frustrated, dying church very soon if he didn't embrace the next generation in his community and his church. He could sense trouble tomorrow if he didn't act today.
At the next staff meeting, Pastor Mel walked into a room full of young leaders and made an announcement: "Today our church will change forever. I will no longer ask you to build a church for my generation but I will help you build a church for your generation. What do we need to do for that to happen?" He could feel the lights switch on for these new leaders.

As theologian Leonard Sweet has said, many over-35s are still trying to make a credit-card call on a rotary telephone. Pastor Mel's congregation had to reevaluate, retool, and rediscover in order to reform their church to be more effective in today's world. They had to reconnect. They changed their values to engaging their culture, living in authentic relationships, empowering people's potential and being driven by compassion. They now call themselves "a small church with lots of people."

How are they doing? Great. Did they lose any "giraffes"? Not one. Is their future brighter than before these changes? Absolutely. Why? Now they have a church that will carry on after they're carried off!

Chapter 39

Busy Waiting or Waiting to Be Busy?

Average people allow time to impose its will on them; remarkable people impose their will on their time.
—Jeff Haden

On a recent trip to South Africa, my wife Becky and I checked into a hotel in Port Elizabeth. I asked the hotel desk clerk if they had Internet capabilities. He replied rather sheepishly, "We are busy waiting for the new Internet to be installed."

That is a great South African expression. We are "busy waiting." I have heard that expression many times during more than 25 trips I have made to South Africa. I'm in no way being critical here. In fact, I am being complimentary. At least they are busy working while they are busy waiting. That is much better than doing nothing until that Internet gets installed.

Jesus addressed the "busy waiting" concept with His disciples in the Garden of Gethsemane. He asked them to wait, stay alert, stay awake, and stay engaged while He was praying. Matthew, one of the disciples, recalls what happened.

"When Jesus came back to his disciples, he found them sound asleep. He said to Peter, 'Can't you stick it out with me a single hour? Stay alert; be in prayer so you don't wander into temptation without even knowing you're in danger. There's a part of you that is eager, ready for anything in God. But there's another part that's as lazy as an old dog sleeping by a fire' " (Matthew 26:40-41 Message).

At this crisis point in His life, Jesus is praying while His church is sleeping. Jesus keeps working inside us while He is waiting for us! He is busy waiting.

Let's face it. We have all been tempted to be that lazy old dog at times. We begin self talk like, "There's no use ... things will not get better ... I'm a victim." When we quit looking for that job in tough times, when we give up, when we just sit at home and become dependant on others, something bad happens. We start to wander into destructive temptations of spirit, soul and body. We lose passion. We lose dignity. We lose life and self-control. We give our power to others. We adopt the habit of waiting to be busy.

Remember that saying about idle time and the devil's workshop?

In an article for Inc.com, writer Jeff Haden notes a better strategy for living in the down time between start and finish:

> "Time doesn't fill me. I fill time."
>
> "Deadlines and time frames establish parameters, but typically not in a good way. The average person who is given two weeks to complete a task will instinctively adjust his effort so it actually takes two weeks.

"Forget deadlines, at least as a way to manage your activity. Tasks should only take as long as they need to take. Do everything as quickly and effectively as you can. Then use your 'free' time to get other things done just as quickly and effectively.

"Average people allow time to impose its will on them; remarkable people impose their will on their time." [lxxxvi]

Hollywood mogul Samuel Goldwyn once said, "The longer I work, the luckier I get." He was busy waiting.

Chapter 40

Motives that Motivate and Motives that Un-motivate

When you're alone on the side of a hill with no one around but a bunch of sheep, you don't get many accolades, except from God.

I want to tell you a true story that happened to a pastor friend of mine. He was single at the time and very concerned about presenting himself in a way that a pastor should when dating a girl. Eventually, he became serious about a godly woman. Wanting to be a good spiritual example, he dated her for many months. Finally, he asked her a question after a long evening conversation. "May I kiss you?" he asked.

She responded, "Why? Why do you want to kiss me?"

Checkmate!

Do you understand what she was asking in her mind? What is your motive? What does kissing me mean to you? Is this love, like or lust? Where are you going with this? Maybe you are single and reading this story. There might be some wisdom for you in using her response, too! It might save a lot of heartache and counseling.

Years ago I heard a leader say that the two greatest Goliaths (as in David and Goliath) of life are attitude and motive. I believe that. More people have problems with these two issues than any other issue I can think of. Today's thought concerns motive.

Motive is a "why" issue. Motive is about character and integrity. Why? Why do you want to be a leader? Why do you want to kiss me? Why do you want to be elected? Wrong motives can ensnare us in ego-driven pursuits, even to the point of actions that compromise our values with the excuse that the end justifies the means.

When God wanted a leader for His people, He chose a guy named David who consistently did the right things for the right reasons. You can read about his three qualifications that resonated with God in Psalm 78:70-72. His first qualification was "God took him from the sheepfold; from the caring for nursing mother lambs and their babies to shepherding His people." This shows that David's motive for shepherding was love. Neither the sheep nor the people of Israel were there for David. He was there for them. As Israel's king, he remembered both the adults and the children, the makers and the takers, and shepherded the whole nation.

When you're alone on the side of a hill with no one around but a bunch of sheep, you don't get many accolades, except from God. Remember, the further we get from real people, the greater the possibility of using people rather than serving people. David had the right motives for leading a nation — love — not self-centered gain and vainglory.

His second qualification was "David shepherded them according to the integrity of his heart." David lived a lifestyle of character and good motives. Think of it:

Bad motive + good management = Foe as a leader.
Good motive + bad management = OK as a leader.
Good motive + good management = Best Leader.

David's third qualification was "Guided them with his skillful hands." David knew how and why to lead. David developed their gifts, skills, and talents. He developed their competency and capacity so they could be who and what God had called them to be. He had good motives (heart) and good management (head) making him a great leader.

There you have it. If you can apply this, you just slew a Goliath!

Chapter 41

Finish Strong Where You Belong!

Remember, you are not racing others so much as racing yourself. It's your race to win or lose. God is always there to help you finish.

Recently I turned 60 years old. I realized that I would like to be among those who finish strong, not wrong. What is finishing strong?

A bit of Internet humor says, "Give a man a fish and he will eat for a day. Teach a man to fish and he will sit in a boat all day, drinking beer." Now don't get it wrong here. Beer isn't the issue. Sitting in a boat all day, every day, to the exclusion of everything or everyone else is. After all, nothing is foolproof to a sufficiently talented fool. Good things, taken to extremes, can become bad things. Extremes can divert us from finishing strong.

Did you know that the Bible mentions more than 1,000 leaders? Dr. Robert Clinton, whose life has been devoted to the art of leadership, has studied almost all of these leaders. From among this group, he has narrowed the field down to 100 prominent leaders. He wanted to know how many finished strong in their personal, family and church lives.

After careful study, Dr. Clinton found that the Bible gave enough information about only 49 of these leaders to determine how they finished. He broke these leaders into four groups: 1) cut off early, 2) finished poorly, 3) finished "so-so," 4) finished well. You may or may not recognize some of the names, but let's try to understand what these four basic categories of finishing life represent for us. In his book Finishing Strong, author Steve Farrar quotes Dr. Clinton's results:

"Cut off early means that they were taken out of leadership by assassinations, killed in battle, prophetically denounced or overthrown. Those cut off early include Abimelech, Samson, Absalom, Ahab, Josiah, or John the Baptist. Some of these leaders were good but most were bad." Most have a rather tragic story that explains their finish.

"Finished poorly means they were going downhill spiritually or in competency during the latter part of their lives. Some who … are typical examples of finishing poorly include: Gideon, Eli or Solomon. In other words, these guys were barely able to crawl across the finish line. Either that, or they were carried."

"Finished so-so means they did not do what they could have or should have done. They didn't complete what God had for them to do." They were pretty good guys like David, Jehoshaphat or Hezekiah but they didn't finish strong. They were in the middle of the pack.

"Finished well means they were walking with God at the end of their lives. They were strong in faith, family, and community." [lxxxvii]

Examples are Abraham, Job, Joseph, Joshua, Caleb, Samuel, Elijah, Daniel, John, Paul and Peter to name a few. This is where you and I hope to be, right?

The first three groups of leaders were as gifted and called as the fourth group, but why didn't they finish well?

Steve Farrar observes, "All of these leaders were gifted and all had very impressive strengths. So how come they didn't finish strong? The answer is this. They all didn't finish strong because they didn't survive the ambushes." He goes on to say, "Getting through ambushes is what separates the men from the boys. And the guys who get through the ambushes are generally the guys who anticipate the ambushes." That's good advice.

Consider King Solomon. Even though he had more wisdom than anyone else in his generation, he didn't anticipate some ancient ambushes. What were the ambushes? He was ambushed by too many women. He was ambushed by money. He was ambushed by a neglected family. Ouch! Many a leader has suffered the shipwreck of betrayal and sex, extreme love of money and being so busy that they didn't invest time with their family.

To tell you the truth, there were consequences to those ambushes. Solomon had over 700 wives and 300 concubines. Farrar says, "No wonder he didn't finish strong. He was exhausted." Solomon had so much money that there was silver lying on the streets of Jerusalem. His money couldn't even be counted. Solomon's wives turned his heart against the Lord, and his son Rehoboam split the nation of Israel shortly after Solomon died. I get the feeling Solomon didn't spend much time with his son.

Let me add the ambush of pride and status. Status-driven people are motivated by excessive pride. A good self-image is one thing. Excessive pride is another. Nineteenth century Scottish philosopher Thomas Carlyle said, "The greatest fault is to be conscious of none." [lxxxviii]

Let's get smart. There are ambushes everywhere. Let's predetermine our choices so we won't have to make our choices in times of boredom, confusion, passion or battle. World War II General George S. Patton, Jr. said, "Untutored courage is useless in the face of educated bullets." [lxxxix]

Life is like a race. It's how you finish that counts. In a football or rugby game, a team can have a weak first half but come on strong in the second half. Some teams start strong, have a terrible second or third quarter, and then win in the fourth quarter.

The same is true in life. If you are living, and I assume you are or you wouldn't be reading this chapter, even those whose life has been so-so in the first, second or third quarter can finish strong in the fourth quarter. Remember, you are not racing others so much as racing yourself. It's your race to win or lose. God is always there to help you finish.

While ambush may open the door to calamity, God's grace closes the door.

So, let us live in such a way that when we die, even the undertaker will be sorry!

Contact the Author

Dr. Ed Delph
Nationstrategy
7145 W. Mariposa Grande Lane
Peoria, Arizona 85383

www.nationstrategy.com
nationstrategy@cs.com

Other books by Ed Delph:

Church @ Community, Creation House, 2005
Learning How To Trust ... Again,
(co-authored with Alan & Pauly Heller)
Destiny Image Publishers, 2007, 2008
The 5 Minute Miracle, Destiny Image Publishers, 2008
Learning How To Trust (Revised & Expanded Edition),
(co-authored with Alan & Pauly Heller) Destiny Image Publishers, 2009
Making Sense of Apostolic Ministry,
International Resource Network, 2002 & 2009
People Who Overcome, 2011

Nationstrategy: Envisioning and Empowering Community and Church Leaders for Societal Transformation and "Upliftment."

Nationstrategy: We Reveal "Mindskins" That Create Wineskins and Environments for Community Transformation and Enhancement.

Nationstrategy is a movement of community and church leaders united for the purpose of uplifting people and communities ... bringing both closer to their God-given purpose and potential.

ENDNOTES

i http://talk.baltimoresun.com/showthread.php?p=2264036.

ii http://udini.proquest.com/view/a-resource-for-assemblies-of-god-goid:856900850/.

iii http://www.iabc.com/awards/leadership/communication.htm.

iv Stan Toler, *Minute Motivators for Leaders,* Honor Books, (Colorado Springs, 2002).

v Stephen R. Covey, *The 7 Habits of Highly Effective People: Powerful Lessons in Personal Life Change,* Free Press, a division of Simon & Schuster, Inc., (New York, 1989, 2004).

vi Quoted by John C. Maxwell in *Leadership Gold: Lessons I've Learned from a Lifetime of Leading,* http://books.google.com/books?id=WTOGHY0HuzkC&pg=PA15&lpg=PA15&dq=a+man+without+decision+of+character&source=bl&ots=3eM6jFW0oo&sig=BLcQ2FzsFNc-xL6HttFCJICgDX8&hl=en&sa=X&ei=-RL2UNzCIMqMqgHVr4CwAQ&ved=0CDMQ6AEwAA#v=onepage&q=a%20man%20without%20decision%20of%20character&f=false.

vii http://www.cybersalt.org/clean-jokes/nephew-caddy.

viiii Maxwell, ibid.

ix J. Paul Getty. (n.d.). BrainyQuote.com. Retrieved January 16, 2013, from BrainyQuote.com Web site: http://www.brainyquote.com/quotes/quotes/j/jpaulgett150859.html.

Read more at http://www.brainyquote.com/citation/quotes/quotes/j/jpaulgett150859.html#MesYZzZmvEyKIlp3.99.

x William M. Boast, Ph.D., *Masters of Change,* Marocome, Ltd., (Denver, 2005).

xi John Huey and James A. Anderson, "NOTHING IS IMPOSSIBLE You can meet any challenge if you recognize a shift in the paradigm. Ready to throw out the old rules?" *Fortune,* http://money.cnn.com/magazines/fortune/fortune_archive/1991/09/23/75501/index.htm.

xii David Kadalie, *Leader's Resource Kit: Tools and Techniques to Develop Your Leadership,* Evangel Publishing House, (Nairobi, Kenya, 2006).

xiii John C. Maxwell, from Injoy Life Club Vol 14, No. 3, "Leadership Paradoxes," (September 1998).

xiv http://www.telegraph.co.uk/finance/2937087/Wal-Mart-unleashes-charm-offensive.html.

xv http://en.wikiquote.org/wiki/Harry_Emerson_Fosdick.

xvi http://www.cybersalt.org/clean-jokes/kitten-revival.

[xvii] John C. Maxwell, *Teamwork Makes the Dream Work,* J. Countryman, (Nashville, 2002). http://www.amazon.com/dp/0849955084/ref=rdr_ext_tmb.

[xviii] http://www.snopes.com/humor/nonsense/typos01.asp.

[xix] http://wordforyoutoday.blogspot.com.

[xx] http://www.icelebz.com/quotes/william_a_ward/.

[xxi] www.inspiring-quotes-and-stories.com/balance-sheet-of-life.html.

[xxii] Albert Einstein, quoted by William Miller, *Life* magazine, May 2, 1955, http://einstein.biz/quotes.php.

[xxiii] Steven P. Ketchpel, Ph.D., *Giving Back: Discover Your Values and Put Them into Action Through Volunteering and Donating,* (2012), http://giving-back.info/buy/.

[xxiv] http://www.examiner.com/article/zig-ziglar-has-passed-away-he-died-today-at-the-age-of-86.

[xxv] http://www.cybersalt.org/clean-jokes/bagel-shop-student.

[xxvi] http://josephmattera.org/index.htm.

[xxvii] http://www.bispomacedo.com.br/en/2011/03/05/the-pig-and-the-horse/.

[xxviii] Loren Gresham quoted by Stan Toler, *Minute Motivators for Leaders,* Honor Books, (Colorado Springs, 2002).

[xxix] Ken Blanchard and Phil Hodges, *Lead Like Jesus,* Thomas Nelson, (Nashville, 2005).

[xxx] John C. Maxwell, from *Injoy Life Club* Vol 14, No. 3, “Leadership Paradoxes,” (September 1998).

[xxxi] http://blog.barnesdennig.com/2008/02/the-5-big-challenges-in-life.

[xxxii] http://memory.loc.gov/ammem/wrighthtml/wrighttime2.html.

[xxxiii] John C. Maxwell and Tim Elmore, The Power of Partnership in the Church, Thomas Nelson, (Nashville, 1999).

[xxxiv] http://www.goodreads.com/author/quotes/23387.Andrew_Carnegie.

[xxxv] http://www.amazon.com/Wooden-Leadership-Create-Winning-Organization/dp/0071453393.

[xxxvi] http://books.google.com/books?id=eEgSVEmn8iYC&pg=PA27&dq=a.w.+tozer+%22what+a+pity%22&hl=en&sa=X&ei=f_v-ULasOKXY2QX_4YHQCA&ved=0CDUQ6AEwAA#v=onepage&q=a.w.%20tozer%20%22what%20a%20pity%22&f=false.

[xxxvii] John C. Maxwell, from Injoy Life Club Vol 14, No. 3, “Leadership Paradoxes,” (September 1998).

[xxxviii] William H. Ewing, *Nimitz: Reflections on Pearl Harbor,* The Admiral Nimitz Foundation, (Fredericksburg, TX, 1971).

[xxxix] http://nomadia.smfforfree.com/index.php?topic=20.195.

[xl] http://www.broadcaster.org.uk/section2/jokes/christianjokes.html.

[xli] As written by Kristin Beers.

[xlii] The four "power" principles in this chapter are from Dr. Mike Murdock, *Wisdom for Crisis Times: Master Keys for Success in Times of Change*, Wisdom International, (Fort Worth, 1992).

[xliii] http://www.reginabrett.com/life_lessons.php.

[xliv] www.crossroad.to/Victory/stories/wild-pigs.htm

[xlv] http://www.connectingforexcellence.com.

[xlvi] Dr. Mike Murdock, *The One-Minute Businessman's Devotional,* Honor Books, (Colorado Springs, 1992).

[xlvii] http://thinkexist.com/quotation/the_past_is_a_guidepost-not_a_hitching_post/213533.html.

[xlviii] Agapeland, "The Music Machine," Candle Company Music, (Dallas, 1977) http://www.agapelandmusic.com/catalog/item/686755/306434.htm.

[xlix] http://www.cybersalt.org/clean-jokes/tennis-ball-lesson.

[l] Mike Murdock, The One-Minute Businessman's Devotional, Honor Books, (Colorado Springs, 1992).

[li] http://www.i18nguy.com/engineers.html.

[lii] http://www.quotecorner.com/Jackie-Mason-quotes.html.

[liii] Steve Ventura, *Lead Right: Every Leader's Straight-Talk Guide to Job Success,* The Walk the Talk Company, (Flower Mound, TX, 2008). http://books.google.com/books?id=Blkxi2pAlAUC&pg=PA48&dq="If+there's+any+concept+that+is+synonymous+with+leadership+it's+got+to+be+responsibility."&hl=en&sa=X&ei=F2MJUZnAA9DVqQH-kYGQCA&ved=0CC8Q6AEwAA#v=onepage&q="If%20there's%20any%20concept%20that%20is%20synonymous%20with%20leadership%20it's%20got%20to%20be%20responsibility."&f=false.

[liv] http://faculty.frostburg.edu/mbradley/psyography/alfredadler.html.

[lv] Kenneth O. Gangel, *Competent to Lead,* Moody Press, (Chicago, 1974).

[lvi] http://www.thespoof.com/jokes/2436/trusting-burglar

[lvii] Mark Knight and Emma Mason, *Nineteenth-Century Religion And Literature: An Introduction,* Oxford University Press, (Oxford, 2006).

[lviii] Warren W. Wiersbe, *Meet Your Conscience,* Back to the Bible, (Lincoln, NE, 1983).

[lix] http://www.jokesclean.com/Age/MoreAgeJokes.php.

[lx] http://www.cybersalt.org/f-16-jokes?Itemid=100495.

[lxi] Luke 10:40-42, Message.

[lxii] http://archiver.rootsweb.ancestry.com/th/read/FOLKLORE/1999-09/0936207690.

[lxiii] http://books.google.com/books?id=rhIFmROSZmgC&pg=PA10&dq=andr

ew+grove+%22understood%22&hl=en&sa=X&ei=n_APUYGyPMS0qgGd0IGQBw&ved=0CC0Q6AEwAA#v=onepage&q=andrew%20grove%20%22understood%22&f=false.

lxiv http://www.cleanjoke.com/humor/Wrong-Email.html.

lxv http://thinkexist.com/quotation/as_i_grow_older-i_pay_less_attention_to_what_men/151029.html.

lxvi Isaiah 1:18a.

lxvii W.B. Freeman, *The Original Inspirational Bathroom Book: Facts, Stories, and Humor from the Good Book,* Warner Faith, (New York, 2009).

lxviii http://www.amazon.com/24x36-Procrastinators-Creed-College-Poster/dp/B000G64IUQ.

lxix http://www.tribuneindia.com/2007/20071124/saturday/webside.htm.

lxx John Mason, *Conquering an Enemy Called Average,* Insight International, (Tulsa, 1996).

lxxi http://forums.di.fm/personal-life-and-relationships/saying-the-right-thing-at-the-right-time-105012/.

lxxii http://www.merriam-webster.com/top-ten-lists/top-10-favorite-quotations-about-words-vol-2/art-of-conversation.html.

lxxiii http://www.orgcoach.net/newsletter/april2005.html.

lxxiv Luke 8:22-25.

lxxv Matthew 6:28-32, Message.

lxxvi Cybersalt.com.

lxxvii http://www.colorado.edu/peacestudies/se/debt/archives/msg00802.html.

lxxviii Jeremiah 29:11.

lxxix http://www.cybersalt.org/clean-jokes/sidewalk-preacher.

lxxx Esther 4:14.

lxxxi David Kadalie, *Leader's Resource Kit: Tools and Techniques to Develop your Leadership,* Evangel Publishing, (Nappance, IN, 2006).

lxxxii http://www.goodreads.com/quotes/289212-don-t-become-a-wandering-generality-be-a-meaningful-specific.

lxxxiii http://www.rinkworks.com/said/samuelgoldwyn.shtml.

lxxxiv http://www.characterfirst.com.

lxxxv http://bibleforums.org/showthread.php/156453-And-I-dare-any-of-you-to-pick-on-me.

lxxxvi http://www.inc.com/jeff-haden/9-beliefs-of-remarkably-successful-people.html.

lxxxvii Steve Farrar, *Finishing Strong,* Multnomah Publishers, Inc., (Sisters 1995).

lxxxviii http://en.wikipedia.org/wiki/Thomas_Carlyle.

lxxxix http://www.generalpatton.com/quotes/index3.html.